Death By Completion
A Guide to Conscious Dying

JoEllen Goertz Koerner
with
Florence Caroline Goertz

DEDICATION

This book is dedicated to my beloved sisters, Paulette and Bernette, and my brother Richard, who helped me learn how to live, and helped Mother learn how to die—and have fun doing it! I also want to thank them for serving as Editor to my life story in general, and this story in particular. They truly give me the lived experience of truth, beauty and love.

CONTENTS

INTRODUCTION

This book is intended for the living—those who are living their life guided by the power of their own dreams and desires. It is also designed to assist those who are dying. It's all the same group! If you follow the principles modeled by my Mother, I guarantee you a most amazing life journey whose outcome is simply—the completion of a life well lived.

Now my Mother, Florence Caroline Goertz, was an extra-ordinarily *ordinary* woman! This is why *what she did can be done by anyone*—even me!! This is a book of hope, of joy, a celebration of the resiliency and creativity of the human spirit. It is a guide to Conscious Living so that we can practice and be ready to engage in the great finale—Conscious Dying. And the time to begin is *now*! You can be young, old, or in the middle. You can be in the prime of health, or in the last days of your life. The only requirement is your *desire* to do your best till your last breath. And, that last breath can be the sweetest in all your life.

Born in 1920, she spent the entirety of her ninety (90) years in a small rural South Dakota community—population 1000. Her world circled around the family and friends of her childhood (they were all related), the church of her heritage (Mennonite), and the role ascribed to her by society (mostly). A woman of that era had the strongly defined role of helpmate to husband, woman of the house, social director of the community, and self-sacrificing mother of the world. She did all of those things with grace—most of the time. If we overlook the occasional meltdowns with her four children (boy, girl, twin girls all born within a 3 year time frame when there were *no* modern conveniences to help with the diapers—and disposable was a dirty word thanks to the Great Depression), she was really QUITE normal!

To those watching our family, Mom did it all—just like the rules said. She taught Sunday School and brought flowers to church. She led the Girl Scout Troop in the community. She supported the huge love of her life—my Dad, in ways that were waaaaaaaaaaaaaaaaaaaaaay beyond what was required. He was a very handsome and brilliant man, intelligent and witty. He was inventive and popular, and a historian besides. Not the dry and boring kind. His stories were always juicy and filled with the little nuances of the human condition (secrets about things people *really* did and said when no one was looking). He always lived by the axiom 'don't let the truth spoil a good story', so he took some limited license with his fables. But for the most part, they were fact! In fact, Augustana College gave him an honorary PhD and took his vast collection of stories and pictures, dedicating a section of their archives to his work. It stands their proudly today—as does the picture of my Mother, beaming at his side. This picture does NOT show her frustration over the countless meals she had to prepare when his friends would drop by to explore his extensive library in their home.

Now, what a simple description of my Mother does *not* display is the enormous way she navigated the world in ways conventional—while also doing her own thing brilliantly, in ways invisible to the non-discerning eye. It was during her dying that I came to fully appreciate all of that. Being a teenager of the 1960's, I had felt the usual disinterest (and occasional dislike), for parents of that era. What could they possibly know after all?? Let me tell you—*plenty*! And, as I walked with her those final few years of her life, I learned more about life and living than all my years in education and service in the healthcare industry combined.

As we spent the last month of her life living under the same roof in her beloved little apartment, practicing principles of Conscious Dying, we had some of our most meaningful exchanges. One day I said to her, "You know Mother, you really should share your journey towards death with others—*it is so inspiring.*" After a deep conversation, she agreed. So, Mother is the author, and I am simply reporting the situation the way I experienced it as a daughter who loved her so deeply. She lived her journey with conviction, courage, authenticity and grace. She agreed to share her story, blessing this effort. If you walk her path with me, you too will know the joy of a life well-lived and a death of celebration and peace—Death by Completion.

1 COMPLETION:
The Act of Conscious Dying

Everything in life exists within nature's framework of birth, growth, death and rebirth. Rather than building your expectations on permanence, realize the inevitable rhythms of change. As you embrace change, you enter into the flow and cadence of life.

Mother had wanted to be a nurse. It was her dream. However, in her little tiny community of 1000 people what they really needed was teachers. So she dutifully got a teachers certificate and taught in a small country school. Each year she would have 7-8 students of assorted age and size, filling most grades. Mom would live in the home of one of those students during the week, traveling to her parental home for the weekend. Eventually she married my Father, left teaching and moved on to the next chapter of her life.

She always remembered that dream of nursing. So after we all left for college, Mom served as a receptionist in the little Medical Clinic in town. People to this day love her for making room for them when a mini-crisis hit their lives. It was in that role of service that she blossomed—her heart was here. *This was her destiny.* It was many years later that I saw how that pattern of service wove itself through her life in such a deep and significant way. It was part of the secret to her wonderful ending (we will explore that in detail later).

I was somehow motivated by her love of nursing; I decided that I too wanted to be a nurse. My first nursing instructor came to me

1

when I was 7 years old. Mrs. Brown lived down the street from our home, age 93, both frail of body and strong of will, and *very* opinionated! She had a tabby cat that needed to be fed, scratched and played with daily. While Mrs. Brown was very capable of the first two functions, it was the third she could no longer provide with vigor. It became my self-appointed task to show up each day after school and take Mittens for a playful romp in the front yard, feed her a saucer of milk, and return her to the waiting Mrs. Brown.

The cat was simply an excuse, a front for my true intent. What I *really* experienced each day after school was the most engaging dialogue with a wise soul who had lived life with enthusiasm while reflecting deeply on its contents all along the way. Her capacity for story-telling was matched by her ability to mine the meaning and implications out of seemingly simple and trivial events. And, as she told her stories, she would 're-member'! Each time an especially treasured memory surfaced her clouded eyes would twinkle, her wrinkled face would light with joy, and her voice would fill with emotion as she recounted this compelling moment in time.

Over time I noticed that every time Mrs. Brown would go through a series of memories her energy would shift, and her whole being became more animated. I could see that by drawing on those moments she would gain strength, vitality, and hope. She literally would transform her aged body into a vibrant vessel of well-being. Mrs. Brown showed me that the true capacity for healing and health lies within the individual when someone bears witness to their life with respect and compassion. Mrs. Brown taught me how to be a nurse.

Through the years I learned many things about the profession of nursing from my educational and clinical experiences. Teachers, colleagues, mentors and friends all have contributed greatly to my understanding and appreciation of the art and science of care giving. But it was Mrs. Brown and Mittens that revealed its true essence— simple authentic presence. It was this function that Mom offered others in her role as Receptionist. It was the role my Sisters would serve in that final week of her life when we sat at her bedside in support of her transition. It is the role *anyone* will fill if they truly support another on their journey through life. It is the function of presence that makes all the difference!

A Story of Completion

Fast forward and I was now a nursing student in a nearby town—four months into the program. We had worked diligently in the nursing lab, testing our skills in admissions, injections, bathing….. And finally, the glorious day came—our first day of clinical! We were going live on a unit! I got dressed in my uniform, first pair of white nylons, a high school graduation gift from an older nurse I admired. My new unused bandage scissors. Anticipation was running high!

Oh dear—I was assigned to 3 North Medical—the instructor who supervised students in this area had the reputation of a tyrant. I received my first assignment, the patient in room 312. My role was to simply admit her and fill out the necessary forms. "Simple enough", I thought to myself.

I shyly tapped on the door and entered her room. This most beautiful woman, age 75, was sitting on the edge of her bed. I was struck by her serenity and presence. After the required introduction, I asked "What brought you to the hospital?" She looked at me with blue piercing eyes, glinting with a bit of humor, and said, "My children". "Oh! And why do they think you should be in the hospital?" I inquired further. "They think I am crazy" she mentioned in an offhanded way.

Immediately the assessment aspect of my brain conjured up a diagnosis of 'mental illness', and smugly I felt I was really 'getting it'! "And why do they think you are crazy?" I continued. "Because I told them that I am going to die." My mind whirls—'Suicide—that's it!' I think to myself. But—something about all of this was almost surreal. I truly looked at her, and there was not a hint of any kind of agitation or emotion other than deep peace.

I began again, as my paper was still blank. "So what are you dying of, if I may ask." "Completion—I am dying of completion", was her soft reply. In that instant I felt this deep shift within my body. I was all

3

of 18 years old, new to this whole field of work, but intuitively I KNEW that I was witnessing something extra-ordinary.

"I'm sorry, but I am not sure I understand. Could you say a little more about that?" I prodded. She went on to tell me about the wonderful life she had lived. She had just made the rounds to all of her children, spending a week with each one of them. On that trip she had taken some of their treasures she had kept for years, as well as a few meaningful things from her own collection. She told them each how proud she was of them, how much she loved them. She had said 'all she had to say.' Then, she went on to explain, she made a list of all the people that she had to touch base with to 'wrap things up'. She itemized things; people she wanted to thank, those she wanted to apologize to, those she had business dealings or financial matters left to finish. She went through each aspect of her life, and put it all in order. So, here was this beautiful, lucid and peaceful woman, expressing deep gratitude for her wonderful life, and a readiness to surrender it all in graceful passing. She had truly done her personal life work.

I went back to the desk where the Instructor was waiting—page empty. When she asked what the patient was being admitted for, I answered, "Death by Completion". Needless to say she was MOST disappointed, critical of my interviewing skills and gave me a double reading assignment in the library in preparation for clinical rotation the following day.

Returning to my dorm room, I was simply filled with the wonder of that exchange. The next day I was assigned to someone else, but I started my rounds in her room. There she was! Sitting in a chair, she was smiling and serene and very much as she had been the day before. I reviewed her chart—all tests showed normal. The next day I returned again, only to find her room empty. When I inquired at the desk—she had died the night before of 'natural causes'.

Little did I know then that the very first patient of my career was setting the stage for the most important and precious patient of my life—my Mother.

Exercises in Completion

The art of completion rests on identifying and realizing our life goals. This is achieved as we develop a high level of self-awareness and an acceptance of the inevitable realities that disrupt our best laid plans. Watching my Mother live her life—with purpose and a deep sense of direction (usually)—I was always startled at how aware she was, aware of both the possibilities in the present moment and the inevitability that death was the only possible outcome. Not knowing the formal word for it, she was practicing the *Art of Integration*—connecting the past with the present, while anticipating the future.

Life Purpose

A KEY to living an integrated life is being clear about your purpose. Society has taught us that only the rich and famous are successful, and the rest of us—well, we are merely onlookers watching them thrive. This narrow view trivializes the power and beauty of the extra-ordinarily ordinary things in life. Quite simply, a great life is one of connectedness, service, integrity, messiness, uncertainty, beauty and brokenness. It is attempting to live calmly in the middle of chaos, productively in an arena of waste, lovingly in a world of greed and self-focus, and gently in a world of violence. This was the life of my Mother. How clear are you about the direction in which you wish to live your life?

Living a Purposeful Life: What is your vision for your life? What do you want it to stand for when all is said and done? Here are a series of questions to pose to yourself, or share with another significant and trusted other in your life:

- Why am I here? What is the purpose of my life? What have I felt called to do, or be, or offer the world?

- What impact does my life have on current and future generations? Am I in some way making it a better world for everyone and everything? Am I living for the greater good? If so, how?

- How aware am I of the fact that all of my thoughts, words and actions have an effect on everyone and everything in the Universe? How can I be more responsible in all I think, say and do?

- What parts of my family heritage and cultural traditions do I feel called to keep alive? Are there memories of the past, either personal or cultural, that I feel called to preserve?

- What from my heritage or culture do I feel must be changed for the positive evolution of the human family, and the Earth?

- Do I have more or less enthusiasm and motivation for living? Why?

- Does the way I am living my life leave me with a sense of peace? If not, what must I do to shift that?

Remember, rather than looking to the 'celebrities' of the world as a role model, look at some of those who have less than you do, and how they thrive. A great example of that can be found on: http://www.bing.com/videos/search?q=koeras+gott+talent This young 22 year old Korean lived on the street since he was age 5. Do you know what inspired him to this greatness? He heard a man 'singing sincerely'. A man who, to this day, does not know how he inspired another with a very hard life to move forward towards his own destiny--simply by being sincere in living his own path. Someone is watching you…and looking for your sincerity. That's all it takes!

Accepting Reality

We all have an understanding, an expectation of how life should work. We make plans. We work hard. We expect certain things, based on rules we have learned from our family, culture and our own deepest desires. Often times we are surprised, disappointed or devastated when something or someone else disrupts our well intended efforts. Learning to stay balanced through good times and bad helps us survive and thrive through the inevitable changes that are part of living.

Accepting Reality: There are three major areas in life that pull us in two directions. These natural trends really have a way of taking us 'off track'. Consider your thoughts and feelings about each of the following, asking yourself on which side of the coin you are most comfortable:

- Certainty: We want to *know* what will happen next as time and life situations rearrange our best laid plans. This creates a tension between the desire for control and the reality of chaos in our lives.

- Permanence: We want things to *last forever*, to be done once and for all, while the cycles and seasons inherent in all of life produces a shift in conditions over time. This creates a tension between the desire for stability and the reality of change.

- Mortality: We want to *live forever* while we know that death is the inevitable outcome. Death is really our friend—it is totally dependable. This creates a tension between the desire for continuity and the reality of endings.

Indigenous Wisdom says that two ends of a paradox are the same thing in extremes. To live a balanced life, you must learn to stand in the center and be able to move to either side with no strong emotional attachment to either. Experiencing both will give you a deeper understanding of life—and yourself.

Balance is essential for survival. Everything is always shifting, so balance is found in a small moment in time and then we move again. Ask your friends and family to share what things give them a sense of balance. See how many of them mirror or expand your own activities that give you a sense of grounding. *Finding the meaning in an unsettling event is the activity that will always create a balanced view.*

When we know *why* we are here and *what* we expect from life, we make conscious choices that move us in that direction—more or less—the direction of living a purpose-full and balanced life. This provides a path and a process for your journey—a Journey towards Completion.

Reflections on Caregiving

The Patient Speaks:
"For me, there is a reverence for life. It means enjoying the sunshine, the rain, a dust storm, walking down the city street, and looking to see the pleasure, to smell the fresh air. It means bringing the country with me to the city. It's working hard in my garden. It's reading a good book. It's being with people I enjoy. It's even being with people I don't enjoy. It's learning to choose. It's learning my life is limited. It's having an obligation not to cause pain in this life, and to ease it for others when I can."

Florence—Patient

The Caregiver Speaks:
"Perhaps few things are more encouraging to a patient than to realize that his growth evokes admiration, a spontaneous delight or joy, in the one who cares for him. He experiences my admiration as assuring him that he is not alone and I am really for him. His awareness of my delight in his efforts to grow has a way of recalling him to himself. I help him realize and appreciate what he has done. It is as if I said to him, "Look at yourself now, see what you did, see what you can do!"

Milton—Psychologist

2 SIMPLEXITY:
The spiral of life

Simplicity is achieved by not adding anything that does not belong to what is already there. Instead of inserting something to make you or the situation better or worse, simplicity does not allow the mind to tell stories, lies or betray. It doesn't pick up things not needed. Not adding something is simple, but not easy.

Have you ever noticed how simple life is for a child? Their wants and needs are few. They KNOW exactly WHAT they want and WHEN they want it! And quickly, often through wrestling with siblings and conning parents, they learn HOW to get it! Ages and stages—the cycles that make up a life—move us from the simplicity of childhood to the complex world of an adult. The older we get the more people and things gather in our life. And, the more moving parts that a system has, the more that can go wrong—or right!

Suddenly, one glorious day, we realize that we are older; we are on the other side of all that complexity. We no longer have the constant demands of children to raise, the job to perform or the organization to support. We have arrived at 'simplexity'—a simple life with the wisdom learned in complexity. Winston Churchill said that "simplicity lies on the other side of complexity". Once things get SO complicated or so cluttered, we make a move to remove what is unnecessary, and simplify again. Only this time we do so with a more discerning eye. We make wise choices, based on what is sacred and important in our life.

When do we decide to make a move or let go of something—especially when it is important to us? How do we know what to discard and what to hold on to? Practicing the art of discernment is more than just making a decision. It's FEELING deep inside that this decision has energy, spirit, and a sense of de-light in it. If we choose something out of a sense of duty, or because we are in a forced situation, the outcome will feel flat and outside of our-Self. If, on the other hand, we make a decision with spirit in it, there is a sense of moving forward to something greater, even if it looks like a step backwards from the outside.

A Story of Simplexity

Mother and Dad had a great love affair for their entire life. It was one of the few marriages I have known to make that claim and mean it! They got married during WW II and lived in the same house on the corner of 7th and Dewald for the 53 years they were together. Those years were packed with living; camping trips, school and community events, church choir, and lots of creative family activities. After Dad died, Mother was at a loss—for awhile. Slowly, after several years of grieving, she suddenly picked up the pieces and moved forward with a resolve not visible while Dad was around and 'calling the shots'.

One of the first times I noticed this sense of purposeful direction was the day this letter came in my mailbox:

My Dear Children,

I love you very much, and I know you love me. This is the way I have planned the rest of my life, and I hope you will honor my wishes.

I intent to live in my home until taking care of it is more than I am able to do. I will then move into a small apartment. When I need to be cared for, I will enter an adult-care home. When I say "this is what I want", I mean it. You may think I'm being stubborn, but please think of me being determined.

I am now 78 years of age, and you know that I have had a wonderful life. I don't want to spoil yours. I insist that you live yours to the hilt. Enjoy your beautiful homes, and the children and grandchildren. Enjoy your spouses and keep the relationship fresh and alive—you'll need each other in your old age.

I do not want to move in with any of you. Please don't try to talk me into it. You have all been so supportive of my many whims and wishes—you have helped me in so many ways. I can't begin to thank you for your concern, your encouragement and love. That is the greatest gift you can give an aging parent.

And when the time comes that I lose my faculties—take care of me as I need to be taken care of. PLEASE DON'T FEEL GUILT PUTTING ME INTO AN INSTITUTION. You have been faithful children, and I'll respect your decision! These are my orders and I insist that you follow them.

I love you all so very much and can now relax because I know I will be taken care of.

Love, Mom

Needless to say, the siblings gathered on the phone, wondering aloud at *what had gotten into Mom*? Why did she send this? This was not like her! Was she not feeling well? Did she know something we did not? What should we do with this request? Honor it of course! We could all sense a 'shift in the wind', but since I lived closest—and this was 50 miles away—none of us was there on a daily basis to see this slowly unfolding metamorphosis of a women becoming more and more her own person.

Mom continued to live in that same house for another dozen years. But these years were filled with activities of a different kind.

She was always the consummate quilter (Mom made over 100 quilts and I think she actually sold 2 of them—the rest were given to an amazing and enchanting variety of people and places—for reasons often unclear to anyone but her). She had always done much with her 'girlfriends' around that craft. Now she was traveling with a bus group, going to concerts, even camping out with friends in a small remote cabin at age 84 to celebrate her birthday! The woman was unstoppable, unpredictable, and totally delightful (if not occasionally frustrating)!

Mom was no small woman—built more like a Sherman Tank. At 5' 1" she was as wide as she was high, and just as generous. The size of her heart totally overshadowed her physical presence. She had this positive 'go get 'em' attitude and was the world's greatest cheer-leader. People would stop by just to get a hug. She was everyone's Grandma—from neighborhood children, to the children of our parent's friends. Her gift of generosity found her the first to invite people in, and the last to say goodbye. And she ALWAYS had a fresh piece of some new recipe she had just tried, waiting in her kitchen if you stopped by.

Suddenly, we started to notice she was 'slowing down'. In her mid-eighties it was no surprise. I would go home and find the house not quite as clean as it once had been. She was having trouble seeing, dropping things, moving slower, and her energy level had dropped considerably. One day she called me and said, "Josey, it's time for me to move. I have to find a smaller place." Now selfishly, I had always envisioned Mom to live in that home till the day she died—the home of our childhood. It was a large corner lot with much sidewalk and lawn care required. Of course she could not live there forever.

This was one of the first times I 'heard my Mother think aloud'. I went home to sit in the familiar blue kitchen with the well-worn table in its midst. As she poured a cup of coffee we explored her current situation and her decision to move. I asked her what it was that helped her make this important decision. She shared her criteria for ALL the major decisions in her life:

"Ibber-gaba"—German saying for: *When it gets too hard you simply have to let it go."*

That was the voice of discernment.

Exercises in Simplexity

You can always tell if someone—or yourself—is integrated, living a balanced life. It begins if we take the time to *choose consciously* when we have to make a decision, choosing things that will move us in the direction of our dreams/desires. Then we must *reflect* back on the experience. Reflection creates understanding and meaning, and a sense of purpose in our life. A GREAT practice to do each night before going to sleep is:

Reflective Practice

Take time before bed to look back on your day. Identify ONE THING that stands out—either because it is so grand or so painful—and examine it. Do the reflective exercise:

- What really happened—not just what I *wanted or expected* to happened?

- How did I feel about it—what were my emotions during and after?

- What did I learn from the experience—about myself, others, life?

- What do I want to do more or less of if/when such a situation occurs again?

People who practice reflection grow and deepen across the life-span, responding to situations from a centered place of clarity. Those who do not will react with the same old pattern of thoughts and behavior over and over again. Reflective Practice is what gives some people 20 years of life experience and others 1 year of life experience 20 times.

Life Giving Choices

In life we have many moments that require decision-making of significance. This decision will change things forever. However, not to make a choice will also be a choice—and often it leads to unintended consequences. Along with the facts about various alternatives, our own biases and selective perspectives may color or cloud the reality of that choice. While looking over the facts, look inside to see if the feelings that go with those options feel like they are 'live-giving' or 'draining'. Mother knew she could no longer keep the home. To move was both a sense of relief and also a loss. Could she find an alternative that would give her what she needed and also what she cherished—smaller, low maintenance space with freedom?

To make discerning choices that will give you the best possible outcome, consider these facts when reviewing your options:

- Does this choice feel right for me?

- Am I interested in where this choice is leading?

- Do I like the people involved?

- Is this choice good for my whole family?

- Does this choice make sense given my stage in life?

- Do I feel morally justified in making this choice?

- Will this choice help me to grow?

- Do I have a chance to be more creative & inspired by what I am about to do?

Focusing on these 'meaning' questions as well as the practical 'who, what, where, when and why' type of issues will help you make a choice that meets both your physical and your spiritual needs. It assures that the WHOLE of you is being considered, and honored.

Reflections on Caregiving

The Patient Speaks:
"What an experience having cancer is. My whole life will be different for as long as I live, and, yes, I am one of those who wants to live to be a hundred. An exceptional nurse at the hospital told me t 'live each day to the max." Do you know what the max turned out to be once I was up and around again after two surgeries in five weeks' time? It was hanging up laundry in the sun with a cat rubbing against my leg."

Sarah—Patient

The Caregiver Speaks:
"We may assume that people are suffering in ways that they aren't….We project discomfort onto people about their helplessness which doesn't necessarily exist, or we fail to see the character of the suffering that really is there…But more significant still are our past experiences facing our own suffering. Here it the next critical issue we need to engage—one that any of us who seeks to help another must confront sooner or later. Keep things simply as they are without adding or taking away."

Dass—Meditation Teacher

3 AUTHENTICITY:
Know who you are

To be in power and flow, you must first be an individual. Self-empowerment lies in authenticity and the ability to see yourself through your own eyes instead of the eyes of another. Take your power and flow within your own individuality.

We all have beliefs and attitudes that shape our view of the world—and ourselves. As a child we are 'taught' what is right and wrong, the right way to 'be' in the world, how the world works. Adult figures ranging from parents to teachers in all walks of life are experts on the truth. Throughout our youth we are putting together a picture of ourselves, and our place in the world under their guidance.

The traumatic teen and early adult years give us another task. We now have to become engaged with the world in meaningful ways through relationships, careers, and community. In the beginning we often try to 'fit in', as we were taught in childhood. But one day we realize that our experiences don't always match what we were told. DeLorian says, "I may have mis-information, but I never have a mis-experience." We KNOW what we learned in a situation, and will trust it more than someone else's advice (which comes from their own unique experience).

The journey of life is towards increasing authenticity—becoming more and more who we really are. Of course we will never uncover the whole of it, but successful aging finds us more and more true to our own inner compass. We increasingly find that our inner world of thoughts and beliefs will match our outer world of actions and relationships.

Depending on the era in which you live, and the culture of your family—coming to know and express your authenticity can be a rather daunting task. Not everyone is interested in your opinions if they differ too far from the status quo. A quick litmus test is to examine if you are the same when being seen as when alone, or if you are, in fact, two different people. When your head and heart, hands and feet all express the same thing—you are being authentic. People can sense that. It is the foundation of trust. Your inner voice speaks with both clarity and gentleness. It takes quiet and listening to the promptings of your own heart to uncover and then stay true to your Self. This is when you start to live an un-divided life.

A Story of Authenticity

Mother moved into a small apartment and re-established herself. Instead of a large home setting on a corner lot, she now enjoyed a small flower garden outside her window and bird feeders to keep her entertained. No more shoveling snow, cutting lawn or going down stairs to wash her clothes. Life was good!

She maintained her connections with the quilting ladies, the church Women's Aide, the Hospital Auxiliary and her favorite—the et-Cetera Shop. This was a Mennonite sponsored 'slightly used' store that also featured hand-made items from mission groups in Africa, India etc. All proceeds made would be sent to mission work around the world. Mom was a clerk and also one to set the price on things brought in by others. Suddenly we all found our homes filling up with treasures of immeasurable worth found at bargain prices—if not always exactly what we needed!!

She had been living this lifestyle for several years when suddenly one day—out of the blue—she announced that she was quitting at the et-Cetera Shop and all the women's groups EXCEPT for her beloved quilting parties. I was surprised! So I decided to go home and see what all that meant.

Sitting in her now smaller kitchen, sipping coffee and eating her latest fattening creation, I asked her, "So Mom, why this sudden decision to cut back on your activities?" She paused for a moment and then said, "Well it's almost winter and it's getting harder to get around, and quite honestly Josey, I don't like being told what to do anymore!" I chuckled at the thought that anyone ever thought they could tell her what to do.

We looked into the situation more closely and the truth was that she no longer felt part of the group. The next generation had stepped in and while 'old women' were respected an accepted by some, others gave them the sense that they were simply 'in the way'.

I then asked Mother a question I had been holding for such a long time. "Mother", I said, "My childhood memory may be flawed, but I honestly do NOT remember you being so frisky and forthright in my younger years. My memory of you is pretty much doing what Dad and the church told you to do. Where and when did you develop this fierce independence?" This was when I heard the 'Jam Story'.

Mom had just turned 70, and Dad was in his prime. His historical (she would call them hysterical) friends would make their journey to his home to tour the local Mennonite Colonies, the rammed earth homes, the cemeteries of the Great Blizzard of 1882. On each occasion Mom would have to cook the meals after cleaning the house—both before and after the visit.

On this particular trip a party of 30 people was coming. Mom asked the Church Ladies to help her feed the group. She prepared meat, pies, cakes, cooked potatoes for potato salad and did all the things any respectable Mennonite wife would do. It was now the third and last day of their visit, and their last meal. They were serving in the church basement and Mom felt overwhelmingly tired and frustrated. As she carried the platter of ham to the last table, a very old grouchy (by her definition) man snapped at her, "And WHERE is the jam??"

She was able to maintain her composure until she got home. Then she went upstairs to the back bedroom and fell on the bed, weeping uncontrollably. An hour later Dad came home and went looking for her throughout the house. He called her name repeatedly but she did not answer. He went outside, came back inside, looking all over until he remembered this room. He found her upstairs lying on the bed in tears.

"Jimmy, what IS the matter?" he asked, all concerned. "This is just not like you!" To that Mom said, "I don't know what is wrong, Reuben. But this I know. I will *NEVER* cook for your people again. I just can't do this anymore." I gasped aloud! I was stunned for indeed, this was NOT *not* like Mom! "So what happened next?" I asked, my imagination running wild.

"For the next two years your father and I struggled. I tried to figure out what was going on but I could not put my finger on it. All I knew was that I had rights too. I was a person in my own right, and not only the wife of Reuben." We explored together how they worked through this difficult time, and that once they both got used to it— their life together improved. In fact, after they got things 'straightened out' they had the best years of their life. Socrates says that "True love occurs between equals", which is just what they had become— two equals sharing one life.

I then told Mom that as a nurse I have witnessed hundreds of women from her age group blossom in such amazing ways once their husbands died. Not that their husbands were bad, they were just—in control, just as society had decreed. So once the husband was gone and their duty performed—it was time to fly! "WHY", I queried, "did YOU do that while Dad was still alive?" She paused and then said, "*I was afraid I would die without knowing who I was.*"

Exercises in Authenticity

The journey to authenticity can be actively pursued at any time; the time to begin is now!

Uncovering Your Beliefs

Discovering yourSelf is best done by careful detective work—looking for clues. When we are born our tribe and its culture forms and informs us. At some point in life the responsibility for discovering our authentic self, stripped of the rules and forms imposed upon us, becomes our primary task. We are then free to maintain, expand or replace the rules that at one time were life-giving, but now may be slowing our own evolution towards authenticity. Explore your core beliefs and attitudes by engaging in the following exercise.

Draw a blueprint of the home you lived in when you were twelve (12) years old. Put into the picture favorite details like a tree, swing set, garden, or pet, that you loved. In the house you may wish to add a favorite chair, details of a room that was especially significant to you; the chair your father sat in, your mothers place in the kitchen, a window from which you watched the world go by at night. When it is complete, in your mind's eye return to that place and try to recall the following:

- Who were the authority figures in your life at that time (teacher, preacher, parents etc.)?

- What were the messages you received about power, money, success, illness?

- What were the expressed expectations for your gender regarding behavior, dress, and career?

- What were those expressed for your siblings of the opposite sex?

- What were the rules for being 'good' and 'bad' and what happened if those boundaries were violated?

- What were the rewards (or punishment) for thinking outside the box, asking questions, doing things different than the norm?

- What happened if you made a mistake?

- What happens when you die?

21

It is interesting to write out the assumptions you hold about gender-related expectations, power, money, success and failure, why people suffer, what happens to bad people, and to good people, thoughts about life and death. You will be surprised by them, and sometimes delighted, if you can muster the courage for total honesty. Take your time with this exercise. Revisit it frequently. Talk to your siblings and close friends. Visit teachers from your childhood, neighbors, relatives and friends to verify and amplify your memories and understandings.

Examining Your Life Transitions

Life is an ever-changing journey. To identify the major changes in your life, how often you made them, and how you handle change, complete the following:

- Make a list of years, starting with the year you were born, through this current year.

- Map out the typical stages of maturing such as starting kindergarten, graduation from high school, your first job etc. (this would include all the changes that people make based on years of age and traditional life transitions).

- Next, map out the situational crisis in your life, the unexpected events such as illness, death, divorce, loss of job, moving to another town, separation from a dear friend etc. (this would include things that one has not planned, it often come as a shock, disrupting the pattern of one's life).

- Explore the pattern of your life. Some people show movement infrequently with the change being deep and sweeping. Others find that there is frequent activity with much dynamic shifting.

- Pay close attention to the white space between moves. While movement is interesting, it is usually the result of something that has been building up to that moment. Therefore, the essence of your lifestyle pattern, choices, activities and outcomes is born in the rich ferment of what you do to prepare yourself for transition in the white space. Some people find that they always go back to school, and then there is a change. Others find that there is an illness which heralds the shift. While still others find that there is no one thing that propels them forward.

- What basic assumptions guide your expectations for life? Where did you learn them? How do you maintain/expand/ transcend them? How are they manifest in your children? Recognize, honor, and acknowledge the power of your family of origin and how deeply it has grounded you for your own life journey towards wholeness.

- Once you have come to recognize and appreciate the unique pattern that is you, lay it alongside the one that emerges as you study your family of origin (later in the book).

Reflections on Caregiving

The Patient Speaks:
"My son had a chemotherapy nurse in the children's cancer ward, whose job it is to search for any available vein in an often emaciated arm to give infusions of chemicals that sometimes last as long as twelve hours and which are often quite discomforting to a child. He is probably the greatest pain giver the children meet in their stay in the hospital. Because he has worked so much with his own pain, his heart is very open. He works with his responsibilities in the hospital as a 'laying on of hands with love and acceptance." There is little in him that causes him to withdraw, that reinforces the painfulness of the experience for the children. He is a warm, open space which encourages them to trust whatever they feel.

And it is he whom the children most often ask for at the time they are dying. Although he is the main pain-giver, he is also the main love-giver."

Amanda—Mother of Dying Child

The Caregiver Speaks:
"A patient becomes my favorite as soon as our relationship allows them to become authentic. They're authentic when they are themselves—be that eccentric or angry, curious or depressed, sad or joyful. I know then that we trust each other. They just about all become my favorite.

Alice—Nurse

4 SURRENDER:
The Art of giving over

Rather than giving over to something more powerful, true surrender is the process of forgetting your self-determined agenda. By creating a void within, through detachment, you become open and receptive, relaxing into the flow of the Universe. The outcome is appropriate and life-enhancing rather than forced and artificial.

We are all familiar with the attraction of a desire—this intense longing for something that will give us pleasure, security, comfort, or meaning. Desire is the motivation that helps us achieve our goals in life. We spend the majority of our waking hours planning, acting, checking out if that was a good decision or not, and moving forward once again—more or less in the direction of our dreams. Over time we develop preference for some things over other, and prioritize things based on what we love, or what works practically speaking.

As our ability to reflect and make discerning choices grows, we add another dimension to the evaluation process. We now start to explore whether we always do what we *really want* to do, whether we can control our emotions by postponing something to allow something greater to develop. We examine how our motivation by desire compares to being motivated by *principle and ethics*.

Then, suddenly one day, we begin to realize that this whole process instills or reinforces a certain type of restlessness or striving. We never quite seem to 'get there', or 'get it right'. As our life increases in complexity, the choices get harder because there are unintended

25

consequences no matter what we choose. We begin to grow weary of 'the game', and start looking for more peace and serenity.

At that point we change the direction of our life. Instead of wanting things, we start to want intangibles like peace of mind, clarity, our own space, quiet. We stop having preferences for most everything, we release swinging emotions and all their attachments, and physical activity slows as we begin to shift focus towards the inner world. On the outside this looks like a loss, but the depth and breadth of the inner world is far more vast than the oceans. The journey inward leads us home to serenity, to peace, to our true Self.

A Story of Surrender

After a long hard winter spring arrived at last, and not a minute too soon. Record snowstorms, temperature lows reaching to -40 F, and extensive ice cover had kept everything locked up tight for way too long. Everyone in South Dakota was getting cabin fever!

It had been an especially long winter for Mom since she had stepped out of so many of her routine activities. But I also noticed that she was not as eager to jump into the car and run to Casey's for her favorite—chocolate ice cream. Everything seemed to be moving slower, things appeared more of a struggle. And the things she used to love only got a casual nod now. I had taken her to the Doctor for her quarterly exam a month earlier, and nothing seemed particularly out of order. Yes, her blood sugar was quite high (she was diabetic), but she had just shared a piece of fresh raisin sour cream pie with friends. Her A1C showed that she didn't always cheat—we were good.

A few weeks after that office visit I was still uneasy by the pattern shift I was sensing, so I came home to spend the weekend, do a puzzle and just plain 'catch up'. She was still struggling and went to bed early that night, so together we decided to stop and see her Physician the following Tuesday.

I remember the day as if it were the first day of my life. It was a particularly beautiful summer day—not too hot or cold. Sun was perfect.

Birds singing right on pitch. Flowers brighter than ever—and lots of them. As I sat in the doctor's office with Mom, I looked over at her and I could literally SEE the loss of energy and life force surrounding her. There was no more vitality, enthusiasm, or spark in her eyes, just a gray color and withdrawn glaze in her sight. When the Doctor arrived asking her, "How are you doing Jimmy?" I heard words that will forever ring in my heart. "I just don't feel like quilting anymore."

Quilting was the lifeblood of this creative woman. Handiwork, embroidery, wall hangings, wheat weaving, knitting and crochet; she had been in these crafts for more than 80 years of her life. She always had a project going. She gave things away so fast (and they were of beautiful quality so people really wanted them) we could hardly see them long enough to admire their splendor. All of her children would send her things surrounding this interest of hers; we all shared in it one way or the other (as our own abilities and time allowed). *Creating* was the hallmark of her trade, the motivation for her life. And she announced she was done. I knew in that declaration that her time for passing was near, and what a beautiful way to let us all know it!

The half-hour visit extended into three as lab work, x-rays, EKG's and other tests were run to determine why she was having this shift in health. The doctor told me to get a few medications and take her home, she needed to rest more. I took Mom home, knowing that she was on the verge of something but it had not quite yet materialized. The next morning at 5:30 AM I was on my way to Salt Lake City for a Board Meeting. When I got off the plane a message was waiting on my phone from my Sister—they had taken Mom to the hospital for more tests. A follow-up call from her physician told me that Mom was no longer safe living on her own. We would have to make a decision regarding her care when I returned.

With a heavy heart I went to Freeman, rushing to the hospital to find her sitting in a chair, looking beautiful in her robe. Only now she was hooked up to an oxygen machine; she was no longer free. An evaluation was done on her mobility, her functional ability and her respiratory capacity. The Doctor told her that the team was coming with results the next day and that she—not any of us—but SHE had to decide what she wanted to do. Then her future would be planned accordingly.

The next morning my sister, Bernie, and I got her all cleaned up, looking sharp for her 'moment of truth'. "Mom, what are you going to say?" we both asked her. "I'm not telling till everybody is here!" she exclaimed with finality. The healthcare team filed into her room. Thanks to technology, we dialed in our sister, Paulie, who lives in Colorado but is always only a heartbeat away, and set the phone on the bedside table in front of her. Everyone circled round as the Physician said, "So Jimmy, this is an important moment for you. You can no longer live alone, but you have options. And we will explore them just as soon as you tell us all what YOU WANT", (emphasis on the last two words).

I looked at Mom so pale, so exhausted, oxygen machine humming dutifully at her side. She sat upright in her chair and declared her request—loud, commanding, resigned. (I found a copy of her 'speech' scribbled on the back of an envelope crunched into her bed clothes in case she would need to look at her notes—and this is what it said):

> "You know in a few weeks I'll become 91 years old. I've had a good life. Reuben and I lived it to the full and had a great time doing it. When I'd get ready to go to Bible Study he'd jokingly say—you're cramming for the finals! I guess the time is here, sooner than I had expected. So my wish is to be kept comfortable. If I need blood or lab work, that's OK. But I don't want dramatic diagnosis and treatment. When my time comes just let me go into the sunset and become a memory."

There was not a dry eye in the room as the doctor said, "That is the greatest gift you could give your family—clarity about what you want. And, we will be sure that your wish for comfort is fulfilled." I then added on behalf of the family, "We want two more things for you, Mom, along with comfort. You will be surrounded with all the love you have given to all of us through the years; you will not be alone. And—we want to also include a lot of laughter and celebration because you have lived an amazing life! Your death certificate will read—Death by Completion."

Exercises in Surrender

In truth, while Dad appeared to be joking about 'cramming for finals', our entire life is preparation for our last ultimate act—the act of dying. The views we hold about health influences out outlook regarding death. Being aware of the beliefs we hold about both lays the foundation for a decision like Mother made. Explore your attitudes about health as a conscious step in deciding what YOU want when end-of-life issues face you and your family. And help others do the same.

Health Beliefs

We all carry definitions and assumptions about a number of things, but one of the most important is our expectations and understandings around health. How we define health shows our beliefs about life and death, and dictates how we take care of our own.

Some people view health as the "Absence of Disease". They are always 'at war' with disease and spend much of their time fighting off a possible attack by using antibiotics, antiseptics, and activities that ward off illness.

Others, like nursing leader Margaret Newman, have a different view of health. Her mother died at age 77 of a debilitating neuromuscular degenerative disease. In the three year period from diagnosis to death she noted something important; the more ill her mother's body became, the freer and open her mind/spirit became. She went on to write a book about "Health as Expanding Awareness." Her view of health is that a person who continues to grow and deepen in understanding is healthy even, especially when death appears. Death is just one more normal aspect of life. Such a world view sees health as a life well-lived, one filled with experiences and opportunities, joys and losses, all the messy things that make it interesting and full of new lessons to learn. It views death as a celebration, a passing to a new stage of higher order.

To uncover the assumptions and expectations about health that guide your life choices concerning your own physical, mental, emotional and spiritual health, consider the following:

- What is the meaning of health (physically, mentally, emotionally, and spiritually)?

- How do you achieve, maintain, and enhance it from a religious, cultural, and personal point of view?

- What makes people get ill?

- Why is the meaning of suffering?

- What is the purpose of death?

While it is never too late to explore these questions, the best time to talk with other significant people in your life—spouse, family, friends—about death is when you are healthy and active! This is the time to also explore other views outside of your culture. By opening up to the many other ways people view health, illness, and death, you and your loved ones will develop a broader view of the meaning of this most important, and inevitable event in your life. Getting *clarity in your beliefs* about death is the first step in making decisions such as Mother made, when you are faced with the same task.

Health Behaviors

A national study by Robert Wood Johnson Foundation found that currently the United States only ten (10) percent of illness is a result of lack of medical care. Twenty (20) percent is related to your genes and heredity, another twenty (20) percent reflects the environment in which we live (physical and emotional). *And fifty (50) percent of your health status is created through life-style choices.* Recognize your own health patterns. Only when they are clear to you can you decide which ones you want to maintain, alter or change:

- How do you take care of yourself to foster and maintain health (nutrition, exercise, stress management, etc.)?

- Where did you learn your health/lifestyle habits and patterns?

- What diseases are in your family 'story' that you anticipate may be a challenge for you?

We all hear multiple stories and studies showing that many chronic diseases are hereditary in nature. Many of us know if our family has a history of diabetes, heart disease or cancer. And, we survey our own bodies repeatedly, looking for signs of it 'showing up' in us.

Native American healer Wanigi Waci believes that health is our birthright. We are already well. What we un/consciously focus on, what we hold to be 'our truth' will manifest in our bodies and our lives. One generation's experience with a specific illness is held genetically and the 'potential' for it is passed on to the next. But you may note that one family member may suffer from it while another will not. It is often a matter of our subconscious beliefs that influence the 'inevitability' of the pattern's repetition in the next generation. It is important to note that it is not only the expectation of the person themselves, but equally powerful, the expectation of other key family members, that will foster the appearance of an expected/dreaded ailment.

If there is a family history of a specific disease process you may wish to complete the following exercise:

- What are some of the issues/patterns in your own life that may have made you vulnerable to an illness event?

- What are some of the challenges, stressors, exposures or assumptions that may have weakened your own system?

- Who also had this disorder in your family of origin?

- What role did they play in the family?

- What were the stressors/supports in their life?

- How did they deal with it?

- What did/not work for them in treating the condition?

- What was their outcome with the illness event?

- How are past family experiences with this challenge un/consciously informing your expectations about this health challenge

Chronic illness is not the only thing we inherit from our family. *How* a person looks at some of the inevitable changes in the body due to aging, or 'wear and tear' from activities of daily living or physical work demands, are also central to our self-image of health. We all know people who suffer ill health in silence, while others greet us with an update on the current status of their constipation or stiff joints. One is inspirational, the other—avoidable.

Looking at Mom from a medical point of view—she was chronically ill. She suffered from obesity, diabetes, hypertension and congestive heart failure, paresthesia, carpel tunnel syndrome from all her stitching activity through the years, increasingly limited mobility due to a fused spine from three back surgeries, and legal deafness (we literally 'watched TV' by reading captions because she could only hear slightly—with hearing aids). Aside from that she was in great health! In fact, the older she got the more animated and engaged she became. She never saw herself as ill and never, ever dwelled on her limitations. She was only 'slightly inconvenienced' by these things that got in her way, and just kept adding devices (hearing aide, walker she affectionately called 'her Cadillac', daily insulin management, phone with a text message that wrote out what the caller was saying so she could read it, etc.). We will explore ways that she kept that attitude (later in the book)—it was one of the reasons people were so inspired by her.

For all her adjustments to her limitations, she DID draw the limit on how far her accommodation of illness would go. Food is one of the most culturally sensitive aspects of our lives. In our German culture food was a primary vehicle for socialization. Many times the best conversation flowed around the family table during mealtime. It was considered impolite to turn down a food offering created by the cook, and Mother's serving size was 'ample' (at her funeral celebration we ordered 'extra Funeral Meat' and the kitchen put twice the normal amount of filling in the sandwiches as our Mother would have wanted)! Meat and potatoes, drowning in gravy were always accompanied by several salads and desserts. And we saved many children in Africa from starvation by cleaning our plates instead of wasting food! Mom cooked, served and enjoyed good food till the last three days of her life. She was balanced!!

Moving into the new millennium with low-fat diets and a decrease in sugar intake almost feels like rejection of our family. And when we gather today we slip back into old customs. Only now there is awareness which takes some of the joy out of the overindulgence that was once so commonplace. It also makes us healthier and kinder to the planet. Learning to see our lifestyle patterns and transcend them can be a lifelong struggle. And some of those patterns learned in childhood—well, like her, we are not about to give them up!

Reflections on Caregiving

The Patient Speaks:
"That evening I went to the nurses' lounge. It was homey. The head nurse could see me with tears running down my face. She asked, "Do you need to talk?" and I said, "Yeah, I need to know more about leukemia." I wanted to know what it was, how it worked, what happens with it. The

thing that impressed me was that I could feel her pain for me. I cried for awhile. For the first time through all this, I cried in front of someone else.

Val—Wife of a Patient

The Caregiver Speaks:
"Patience is not waiting passively for something to happen, but is a kind of participation with the other in which we give fully of ourselves. It is misleading to understand patience simply in terms of time, for we give the other space as well. By patiently listening to the distraught man, by being present for him, we give him space to think and feel. Perhaps, instead of speaking of space and time it would be truer to say that the patient man gives the other room to live; he enlarges the other's living room, whereas the impatient man narrows it."

Milton—Doctor

5 FINISHING:
Wrapping up loose ends

Experiencing and expressing your highest nature through your life and work is accomplished through right relations and creative struggle. Friction— the struggle between right and wrong, success and failure— is the refinement of your physical self and your spirit; it is the path of an authentic life. Creative self-expression requires a balance between your independence and your interconnectedness in all that you think, say and do.

What does it mean to be in 'right-relationship' with all things in our life? Enduring ethical and cultural traditions ranging from Native American Spirituality to Judeo-Christian Belief Systems, share the idea that an ethical guidance system serves and supports the well-being of the earth's entire community of life. People and societies, practicing 'right relationships', create systems where the greater good is served for everything and everyone living in it.

Wrong relationships create the breakdown of life-support systems world-wide. Negative attitudes of greed, ego, selfishness, anger and fear, cause economic, ecological and social calamity for future generations. This fosters deep suffering – the misery that comes of poverty, inequality, and hopelessness.

When we place higher values of respect, cooperation, equality and caring into the forefront of our thoughts, decisions and actions, a grand connection occurs between people and their own bodies, people and others within their community, people and material things, and people with the earth itself. The future of the world and every-thing upon it is supported and sustained in a meaning-full way.

Living our personal life in this way supports the life and oppor-tunities of seven-generations. The Lakota Sioux believe that your life and energy impacts/radiates out and influences in the following way: YOU are the 4th generation. Going backward, what you think, do and say impacts your parents, grandparents and great-grandpar-ents. Going forward, what you think, do and say impacts your chil-dren, grandchildren and great-grandchildren. So it is important to be conscious about your life; you live for a world bigger than your own. Make right relations with everything before you leave this earth, and you leave everything—*especially your family of origin*—in a better way.

A Story of Finishing

After Mother's statement about being kept comfortable, the Social Worker, Physical Therapist, and Respiratory Therapist joined the Doctor in explaining her options: moving to an Assisted Living Facility where meals and laundry would be provided while she main-tained mobility and independence; or Nursing Home Care where she would have all care needs provided, but no more true independence.

Mom was frightened, exhausted, and not sure of just how strong she really was. This turn of events had been so rapid that she was dis-oriented—as were we all! As everyone sat around giving their input and suggestions I could sense her despair. WHAT was she to do? If she went to Assisted Living and could not keep up, she would have to move. How soon would that transition occur? And what were the penalties to this approach?

Her empathetic physician assured her that there were no fast rules. She should try what she was comfortable with and if it was not successful, she could move to the next level of care. The Social Worker had checked; there was room in both facilities.

As a nurse of many years experience (not telling just HOW many—you can't count that far), I had seen this scene repeatedly. If you remember nothing else of this story, PLEASE REMEMBER THIS—the *worst mistake* so many well-intended families make at this point in the journey is rushing into a decision and moving the person directly from the place the options have been stated (doctors office, hospital bed etc.) to the facility. ***UNLESS OTHERWISE CONTRAINDICATED, TAKE THE PERSON HOME FOR A FEW DAYS TO GET THEIR THOUGHTS AND LIFE TOGETHER—IN THE COMFORT OF FAMILIAR SURROUNDINGS.*** This little pause in the page gives everyone time to explore all their options and make the best long-term decision.

And that is exactly what we did. My sister and I dressed Mom, rolled her and her new best friend 'oxygen tank' right back home to her little apartment, the center of her world for all these years. In the comfort of her own surroundings, resting in her favorite brown chair, looking out at the humming birds visiting her feeder, she would quiet her whirling mind and find center. From this vista all of us could help her make the right decision. Once she was clear—the rest would be simply another step in her journey.

It is a *very difficult decision for anyone to make*—where to go next when going home is no longer an option. This juncture closes off any possible future for 'the good old days' (not that they were always that great—but funny how the mind works—suddenly we recall all the glorious things in our life, and 'conveniently forget' the lesser moments). Moving quickly from health care facility into new space without the opportunity to go home and tie up loose ends robs the person of closure. Forever there is a gaping wound in their psyche; a part of them is abandoned 'back home' and a marginalized 'self' enters the new world—missing the better part of their-True Self.

And so, we ushered Mom back into her space, new oxygen machine humming not-so-quietly in the next room as the 25' tether of tubing gave her room to maneuver. That first night, we all cried together, laughed together, and simply gave in to the moment. The next day, however, it was time to 'get going'! Mom had important 'finishing work' to do!

I revisited the 'Death by Completion' story and reminded her of 'the list' that the patient had worked through. Mom nodded in agreement. Yes! She had people, things, and affairs to get in order. Only, truth be known, as we sat with her—she opened up one box/folder after another, and there—in true Jimmy fashion—were her plans!

She had all of her financial affairs in one folder, with the key to her bank box etc. intact. Another one held her insurance papers, her social security and Medicare card as well as pharmacy card and related health materials. We also discovered that after Dad passed away she had taken a very small bit of cash and, calling it her 'mad money', she started playing with the Stock Market. Later, after her death, we met with the young man who managed this tiny cash investment. He confessed that she (at age 90) may have had the smallest investment but SHE was his favorite client. He would travel to Freeman to visit, get a baked treat at her table, and relish in her observations about life coupled unbridled excitement when the smallest growth in invest ment would occur. He called her 'Vintage—One-of-a-Kind—words that you usually reserve for a very old and valuable Corvette! And, she was all of that and more!!

In a funny way, I had almost expected the files full of documents. But honestly, that little slush fund of investments really cracked me up! It explained why so often we would watch game shows on TV where people would gamble what they had earned for the bigger award, and she would chuckle with glee when they 'put it all out there' for the Grand Prize, whether they won or not. *Mother was a gambler!!* Let me be precise—a Mennonite Gambler—and if you know *anything* about that faith—well, this was way over the top! May each of us have a bit of larceny in us!!

The file that both surprised and moved me most deeply was the tin box that held her plans for her funeral. In her quiet, reflective moments, Mother had written her obituary, a thank you for the paper, selected her songs—including a copy of the sheet music of the solo she wanted sung at her funeral (she did not want to take a chance that another version of the song might be selected by mistake—mother was a music affectinado). She had written notes to us about the kind of an experience she wanted to be watching from that loftier place in the heavens. It was maybe the most loving thing she ever gave to us, her grieving children. May I learn to be as thoughtful in my own life!

Exercises in Finishing

As we ponder the ending of our life, there are two domains that must be considered: the physical aspects of life that involve interactions with organizations, systems and groups. The second, more subtle, and more difficult, is the list of individuals that we want to reach out to in that personal way for various and assorted reasons. Let us begin with the easier one.

Physical Planning for End-of-Life

Mother had a file for every major category of activities/services she was involved with. Her first entry was made when she turned 78, and the latest edits were placed into the box after her 90th birthday party. Legal things most important for family upon your death pertaining to health and finances include:

- A *living will* which alerts medical professionals and family to treatments you want to receive or refuse, and under what conditions. A legal form is provided for completion by you, and is best completed early in life. This will only be put into effect if/when you meet specific medical criteria and are unable to make decisions on your own.

    o Note: Mother had donated her organs, but due to age and the debilitating nature of her chronic condition, the organs were not harvested.

- A *health care power of attorney* which will name a spouse, trusted family member or friend to make health care decisions for you if you are unable to do so. This document is also referred to as a health care proxy, appointment of a health care agent or durable power of attorney for health care.

- A *care delivery method* determines the type of care you may be choosing when end-of-life appears; explore the three most common options available:

  o Aggressive Intervention: the request to have everything possible done to maintain life

  o Palliative Care: treats people suffering from serious or chronic illnesses, focusing on symptom management; pain, shortness of breath, fatigue, constipation, nausea, loss of appetite, difficulty sleeping, mobility impairment. A multidisciplinary team helps patient and family understand various treatment options as they become necessary. The goal is to relieve suffering and provide quality of life for both the patient and their family.

  o Hospice Care: provides end-of-life care by health professionals and volunteers. They offer medical, psychological and spiritual support to help people dying to have a peaceful and comfortable death with dignity. Pain control attempts to keep the person as alert and comfortable as possible. This care is usually offered when the person has less than 6 months to live, and can occur in multiple settings.

- A *durable power of attorney* covers your financial matters. It begins when you sign it, and stays in effect for your lifetime unless you cancel it. You must put specific words in the document stating that you want your agent's power to stay in effect even if you become incapacitated. The most important element in managing your financial affairs is assigning the role of representing agent to someone you trust (usually a trusted spouse, family member or friend).

You'll want to write a letter for your file addressed to the person most likely to take over your accounts if you become unable to manage your own financial affairs or after you die. (It's a good idea to also send one to them at the time you write it). This could be your spouse, adult child or other relative, your attorney, or the person you have selected to administer your estate. Your wishes can change over time, so it is good to revisit your instructions every couple of years or when your circumstances change. You don't have to follow any legal format. The letter can be handwritten or on your computer.

Things to include that help your family or estate administrator include:

- Name and phone number of your employer, attorney, financial planner, insurance agent, stock broker

- List of your pension plan, bank, brokerage, or retirement accounts

- Instructions on how to get in touch with any of your beneficiaries to your accounts

- Instructions on location of your important documents: Social Security statement, birth certificate, will, trust, deeds, life insurance policies, income tax returns, citizenship papers, marriage license, divorce decree, or military discharge papers

- Information about any debts, such as your mortgage, credit card accounts, or car loans

- Deposit box, bank, box number, location of key

- Computer documents, file names and passwords

Things to identify that will help your family manage this information when you are gone:

- Always sign and date each revision to eliminate confusion over which is your most current statement.

- Make several copies, keeping one with your will and another in a place your family would look first. Don't keep the document a secret! And don't put it in your safe deposit box, where it might be difficult to reach.

Relationship Planning for End-of-Life

Tangible assets, things we can touch, feel and count are the first step in 'finishing touches'. However, they are a prelude to the things of Spirit that make that transition easier or harder in the long run. Once we have our life affairs in order, it is important to take inventory to our human relationships and wrap up loose ends there as well. Research shows that when we have released resentments, fears and anger, our death is easier, and the grieving process for those left behind is similarly impacted.

- Compose a list of people who most positively impacted your life: While the list may not be long, it is one of the most important you can imagine. Reach back into your memory and identify the people who stand out as making the BIGGEST CONTRIBUTION to your life. This will not be hard, for they will pop out of the recesses of your mind quickly. It may be your first grade teacher, a mentor or friend who introduced you to new life-giving ideas, someone you met briefly, for only a moment, but you remembered forever.

- Compose a list of people who most hurt you in your life. Make sure that they are   disappointments or betrayals of magnitude, not the petty every-day variety of grievances. Each of us has these encounters—they are part of the human experience. Find something positive from the experience (remember that in every good event there is something negative, while in every bad event, there is something good within) so you can truly forgive. If the person is still living, you may wish to express that. Or, you can simply release the negative emotions by having a conversation in spirit with the person.

- Now comes a difficult, and very important group of players in your life story. Compose a list of all the people that you have seriously wronged, betrayed, or wounded in your lifetime. This is also the human condition; we do not get through life without doing this. It is important that you ask them for forgiveness in a manner similar to the way that you forgave.

- Finally, now *forgive yourself for being human*. Reflect on all the good things you accomplished in your life, the numerous people you have supported, helped, influenced in a good way. And, remember that the TRUE path of learning occurs as we move both on and off our path. Sometimes our biggest mistakes were our deepest learning. As we truly come to understand this, we develop compassion for the world. *In right relationship we become a healing presence in the world. THIS is the secret of Completion.*

When we can look at all the positives and negatives in our life— those inflicted by other as well as those we inflicted on others—with no strong emotions, but rather gratitude for the lessons and blessings that came from each, we have reached the stage of compassionate detachment. It is the key to surrender and transition.

Reflections on Caregiving

The Patient Speaks:
If it's been too long since you were able to laugh, to relax with a friend, to spend quiet moments in a natural setting, or to have someone lovingly prepare a bowl of soup for you, now you must stop being a martyr. Take time out of caring for me, and tend to yourself. Who can you call right now to schedule a few hours replenishing your strength and maybe even having a good time? If the first person you call is unavailable don't give

up. Who is your second choice for someone whose support can help re-new your energies? Who is your third choice? Make sure you don't give up until you find someone who can join you in a few hours of sustenance and renewal."

Jane—Dying Patient

The Caregiver Speaks:
"Trust is living in patience, knowing that a process greater than your own is moving through all. It's the hallmark of being in perfect alignment with everything around you. It is an activity outside the mind. Your mind is always in time, structured around expectations and rules. Respect, rela-tionships and right timing, things outside of time and mind, are required to achieve the desired results."

Alexis—Therapist

6 REMEMBERING:
Reconnecting with Loved Ones

Expectant waiting is the hallmark of living into our vision. It is a time to hold the future dream strongly and securely with an expectancy of greatness. It allows all the space and time needed for manifestation. Simplifying our inner world allows use of the right amount of energy to enable the change gracefully.

Memory is a wonderful thing! It means we don't have to start from the beginning each moment of our lives. Recollection of some person, place or thing is a commonplace activity in our busy action packed lives. When we remember something we bring a thought to mind (a dozen = 12) or we call it into our mind again (it's your birthday!). This type of memory implies that we thoroughly understand what is to be remembered either through analysis or memorization—the most common forms of learning used in formal education today.

A second form of re-membering occurs because of a deep personal connection with the thing being called forward. We reestablish membership or connection with something of personal value or importance. It is much easier to remember something we are interested in than some boring, abstract or irrelevant piece of data.

Attaching images, whenever possible, intensifies our memory. When we can picture the item under recall (a past lover) the memory also stirs a feeling, adding an emotional element to the memory. Sight (pictures), sound (golden oldie songs), and scent (the smell of a cigar or certain type of cologne) are all triggers for touching back into a past event—positive or negative.

Research shows that over time, the negative memories fade while positive ones live on forever. Aging also shifts the focus of our memory from current issues and events to those of our past. In part we remember them because they were first in our brains 'memory book'. We also increasingly find that we have less in common with current affairs and the people leading them (all the 'old' actors/singers/politicians/leaders/family members are gone). The trends and issues of the day seem foreign (HOW do you work an iPad?). Older memories are comforting, reassuring, and familiar. We reduce the amount of material to work within our own self-made memory system, and suddenly—we remember everything we need to know!

A Story of Reconnecting

Mother was taken back to her home to help her stabilize and make the best decision she could for her new reality. My sister Bernie helped get her settled—and my sister Paulie kept clarity about the issues facing us all during her daily 'check-in' calls with her well-honed intuition and well-timed sense of humor. What would one do without family at a time like this? We went to the Assisted Living facility and found a room that would be Mother's new home if she we able to remain mobile. After Bernie left, Mom and I sat at her well-worn kitchen table to map out her 'next steps'.

I looked into her beautiful face and smiled. She had experienced eye surgery the day before she went into the hospital, so her left eye was widely dilated. When she was weary her eyes held a glazed look. But when she was present that left eye popped wide open—and right now, she was here!

"Mother", I began, "your body has not yet stabilized—it continues to swing between a good day and a bad day". On the good days she could ambulate easily, life was good. On the bad days she barely got out of her chair, life was hard. I continued, "I suggest that we wait to see which way it will go before you move into either setting. And if you would like to practice Principles of Completion, I have several assignments for you".

Mom quickly agreed that she was just not sure how strong she was because her body was not consistent in its strength and resilience. Then her attention shifted to the second part of my comments by asking, "And just what would I have to do for that completion thing Josey?" Truly I was not sure myself, but from all the years of studying holistic healing and integrative medicine, birthing and deathing processes, and working with several Indigenous Tribes, I had a theory I invited her to help me test.

Now Mother's 'gambling instinct' went beyond money. She was always experimenting with her cloth creations and her cooking concoctions (she had better luck with fabric than with eggs and milk when she veered from the recipe). She was eager and excited, "let's try these ideas"! So I began, "Much of society today has this image of dying; one's body gets old, or gets disease, and waits passively to die—often in an institution. In other cultures, Mother, there is a belief that if you complete all of your life work in a good way, you can actively surrender and move on without long periods of waiting and suffering. You work with your body's own wisdom, and let it release you in the good and natural way that was intended when human life was designed. So we have to consider two things. First--what do you want to 'do' to manage your comfort; what measures will you take to maintain and best serve and support your body *without* interfering with its own wisdom about how to release you in a good way? And what will you 'do' to release your spirit from your body by making alignment with things on both sides—where you are now, and where you are going?" The key to that is re-membering who and what you love most and moving towards it in a heartfelt way.

I pulled a paper napkin out of the holder and doodled a 'list' of things Mom could consider that would help with her transition:

- Take only the things her body really wants, whether its food, water, oxygen or medications, as her symptoms shift and change

- Identify two-three people whom she is most eager to meet when she reaches heaven

- Name the things she loved most that she wanted to gift to others important in her life

- Create and complete the 'who and what' list of things to do to finish up (elsewhere in the book)

- Practice breathing and relaxation exercises with her whole body/mind/spirit

- Laugh at all the silly things we would encounter in the days ahead; keep her sense of humor

The other thing we were going to do was begin to sort through the material things she loved most—her treasured possessions—and decide what she wanted to do with them. (When energy is limited, do not have people sort through old things as in 'cleaning'....that will be done later, after they are gone, by those left behind. Save their energy for deathing, and focus their mind/spirit on the beautiful things in their world, not old worn out trivial things)

She started asking for specific quilts, cards, pictures—and with that—our experiment in 'Death by Completion' was launched!

Exercises in Reconnecting

Each of the items on her assignment list was significant, but we started with the one that had most meaning for her; naming the people she was most eager to see. Depending on who you are, or who you are supporting, help them prioritize the list by level of importance for them and move in that order. But be sure to address all of the items. And remember, *ENERGY LEVEL is the guide as to how much, how often and how deeply you will assist the person with completing these exercises.* Be sensitive to their level of fatigue, and stop the minute they lose interest or capacity to focus.

Physical Activities

The physical body is a miracle—your unique spot in the universe. You alone occupy that space! And, the body is comprised of the most powerful pharmacy in the world. You always have everything you need for healing (or dying) within yourSelf unless the situation involves trauma, or emergency. Most things that disrupt the body are slow to develop (including cancer, diabetes, obesity etc.). When you put the body in its best possible light, it will resolve its own issues over time with proper nutritional support, hygiene, activity and rest.

- At end-of-life, often well intended healthcare professionals and family members introduce things into the body that confuse its natural processes, lengthening the dying process. Small things like water or high levels of oxygen at the wrong time can keep the body's 'natural mechanisms' from turning off bodily functions, keeping the person trapped within. One of the most compelling reasons to introduce Palliative Care or Hospice Care into the life of the failing patient is that it prevents unintended consequence from happening.

  o *Following the lead of a person's body in what it wants, and what it needs for comfort only, is essential for an uneventful transition. Listen to the patient's requests. Offer food, water, a bath or back rub, mouth care, but if/when there is no interest do not insist on their engaging these things to make yourself feel better. Respect for each person, and the wisdom of the body is a vital element in Death by Completion.*

- Breath is important. Taking our first breath at birth, and exhaling our last breath at death are the two most important acts the body will ever perform. We are all familiar with the

'Natural Childbirth Coaching' a pregnant mother gets for assisting with delivery of the baby. By utilizing proper breathing techniques, the body is relaxed in certain ways at just the right time to assist with the baby's passage into the world. In similar fashion, breathing patterns can assist the spirit to pass from the top of the head of the body back into its true home.

Assist the patient to practice deep breathing exercises. These slow, deep breaths should be accompanied by relaxation of the whole body, allowing the body to sink deeply into the mattress or the chair, in total rest and repose. At the same time, encourage the person to hold images of floating like a cloud, getting lighter and lighter as they breathe deeply. When the breath is deep and slow, the body totally relaxed, and the mind floating, they are building a pathway for their spirit's transition.

Psychological Activities

While decisions about 'body care' are important, the ones most interesting and compelling to Mother were those of 'spirit care'. She immediately picked as her first assignment selecting two people she was most eager to see (more than 2-3 is more than a weary mind can hold in focus—even a non-weary one will struggle).

- Mom lost her mother when she was 10 days old, so she selected Dad and her Mother as the two people she was most eager to meet in heaven. I brought her the book "Heaven is Real" by Todd Burpo and Lynn Vincent, the compelling story of a little boy who died and returned to describe heaven from his perspective. One principle in the book was that adults in heaven are in mid-life bodies; *no glasses* (I can't wait)! So we found a picture of her and Dad in their mid-thirties. It was a beautiful and happy picture. I placed it prominently in the stand beside her chair, and each day would put a fresh flower beside the picture, surrounding it with beauty. She would frequently be caught staring at it with a smile.

Each night as mother went to bed, I encouraged her to strike up a conversation with Dad and Caroline, her mother. She was encouraged to imagine what they will look like and how she will want to greet them. I asked her to think of the things she was most eager to ask them, the thing she wanted most to share with them. In this activity she was beginning to align her mind/spirit with those waiting on the other side. She was telling them that she was coming, inviting them to be there to greet her. This gave her great joy and a sense of connection as her visualization and articulation of the upcoming transition deepened.

- Maintaining a sense of humor is vital in this process. Throughout the last days of Mom's life we played practical jokes on her. We would laugh at lapses in her memory and our own. We made fun of her problems with gas and GI distress. The little every day things of life are perfect material for silliness. And, of course, she gave it right back to us! In some amazing ways, humor was the easiest part of the assignment!

Laughter is good medicine.

- Re-membering does not only involve reconnecting with loved ones whom we will soon see. Transition is also enhanced by remembering and celebrating the people and events that have given joy and meaning to our lived experience all along the way.

Ask the person where their most treasured pictures and papers are stored. As energy permits, bring out the old photo albums and other documents, letters and books that are most mean-ing-full to them. Pull out things stored that were 'saved for the children'; homemade cards and greetings, gifts made in school, favorite things that the children had given them through the years. Reread old letters from friends and others significant in their life. This form of life review will help them recall positive times of connection with people through the years. A mini-celebration occurs each time a memory returns.

Exploring the treasures we have acquired throughout our life journey gives us a chance to identify what is important, fostering a sense of accomplishment and appreciation. It also helps identify whom we might like to leave them with when we are gone.

Reflections on Caregiving

The Patient Speaks:
"It was in the darkness that I found the light. I was in the pain that I found the gain. It was in the dying that I found the life. It was in the aloneness that I found the need of prayer. And it is through the love of God that I found meaning in my life."

Susan—Patient

The Caregiver Speaks:
"Health is not equivalent to happiness, surfeit, or success. It is foremost a matter of being wholly one with whatever circumstances we find ourselves in. Even our death is a healthy event if we fully embrace the fact of our dying...the issue is awareness, of living in the present. Whatever our present existence consists of, if we are at one with it, we are healthy.

Elizabeth Kubler-Ross—Doctor

7 GENERATIVITY:
Intergenerational Healing

The inner place of silence and observation is your true nature. Each human path is unique; your answers are not others. Observing from and staying within your center without being swayed by the conditions in another's life helps them find their way back 'home' to their own core self as you deepen your own.

One thing in human life is a constant, a guaranteed presence—relatives! Each of us comes from a family-of-origin. The very act of being born assures us that our family is comprised of three cohorts of relatives: our predecessors, those ancestors who have gone before; our offspring, those who will follow after us; and our contemporaries, those we are living with right now—in this moment! A second guarantee is the fact that we will experience the solidarity of connection and the conflict of struggle over unavoidable differences between the generations over time.

The contract between generations is changing as social structures and cultural values shift. What was important to our grandparents does not even exist in society today. We do have running water and fast moving cars so the hitching post for the horse has disappeared. Multiple threats to the traditional family/social unit are also growing. An aging society places increasing care giving demands on other family members. Economic downturn finds younger family members unemployed or underemployed, forcing them to return home for shelter and support. The declining fertility rate has created fewer employees who must now support more elders in the community.

Illness rates and 'fixed attitudes' of many elderly make greater demands on the youth in society. The 'family unit' as once defined has been replaced by multiple life style choices which are shifting the composition and functioning of the 'modern family'. A number of conflicting forces surround this ancient institution.

But looking closer, we also find continuity of certain family behaviors within the changing structure and functioning of the family unit, as well as the larger society. Within the inevitable cycles of change, studies show that relations between the generations within a family (the one we are born into or the one we create), in all parts of the world, remain solid and rewarding. When things get difficult, people intuitively turn to family. A great deal of mutual support is taking place at home. This is primarily due to; the presence of faithfulness and loyalty within the family unit, a give and take in the actions and decisions of different members within the group, self-sacrifice of individual family members for the greater good of the whole, and support by the group of each person's expectations for their own future. In a healthy family ongoing reciprocity is practiced—the cyclical activity of helping and being helped by others and the larger extended family throughout life.

The progression of each generation throughout history indicates that society has always been able to adapt to changing internal and external forces that threaten to divide its members along various lines. Events that occur in the economic, social and political areas outside the family unit will influence the fate of future generations. The process of aging and succession planning (who in the next generation does what; who serves what function within the family and society) will also determine the fate of intergenerational connection. But the one sure thing that will move it towards a dynamic and viable future is a committed effort of all people in the family—today. Remember and celebrate the contributions of those who have gone before and practice principles of cooperation, forgiveness and celebration amongst current family members. Engage in thoughtful and supportive relationships that allow future generations to move towards the dreams of their heart. Cooperation today determines the destiny of future intergenerational relationships.

A Story of Generativity

Now Mother had an unusual life; she lived in one tiny Mennonite community for all 90 years of her existence! She and Dad moved an old home onto the corner of a lot owned by her Father. Through the years the land between her home and his was filled with little houses that her Aunts and Uncles moved into. In a short period of time the whole Waltner family filled one city block. Neighbors were family and their word was their bond.

While that sounds all nice and tidy, it did have its down-side as well. X-ray eyes lived behind the window curtains. The level of grass allowed on the lawn in summer was measured as carefully as the amount of fabric needed for the next quilt. One for all and all for one meant both support AND conformity—Mennonite style! While that was the downside, no one ever did without. Sharing of time, resources, and support for family needs were balanced with multiple moments of play and celebration. Quilting parties, butchering days and holidays were a time for gathering, remembering and celebrating. Her ancestry was always just a step away.

Through the years we, too, lived in and experienced 'the block'. We were always visiting Grandma's house down the street. How often did we do this? Let me tell you a story to show how this neighborhood, not just the house on the corner of 7th and Dewald, was our home.

We had a favorite parakeet, green and messy in her eating pattern. We gave her a very original name—Tweedy. Now Tweedy did not know she was a bird; she thought she was human. She never ate in her cage, always present at the table nibbling crumbs we would obligingly toss her way. She ruled the entire kingdom, including her favorite family member, Rags our Pomeranian dog. Tweedy would hop on his back and ride around the house with him as obliging chauffer.

On this fateful day we were running late for school, rushing to gather up our things. One of us carelessly left the door open, and as we bolted down the street we heard a familiar 'tweet tweet' song. Gasp! Tweedy had flown out of the house and up into the neighbors tree. Fearfully we called, trying every imaginable way to capture this beloved, though obnoxious bird—with no luck. Time had run out, so tearfully we raced off to school, heartbroken at the loss of our beloved pet.

We dreaded going home to an empty bird cage when that very long day ended. To our total surprise, as we walked in—there was Tweedy riding around her great steed Rags! After we left for school Tweedy flew down to Grandmothers house. Grandma was out in her garden when she heard the familiar 'tweet tweet' sound. She recognized the bird, made a strategic call to Mom, asking her to bring Rags to her house. As Mom approached Grandmothers home the bird saw the dog, and jumped on his back. Grandma calmly opened the door and invited Rags inside—for the millionth time. Dog and bird entered together, got swept up in loving arms and were both returned to the safety of our home. Now THAT is famili-arity!!

Family had been the totality of Mother's life. At 90, only her sister Joyce remains. Joyce traveled to see Mom when she came home from the hospital and their shared visit was a strategic door-opener for the reconnection with the family of her childhood which soon followed.

Mom had been experiencing deep loneliness a great deal of the time. I don't mean just lonely like "I miss you". It was more like a displaced person, "I miss simply everything about my 'former life'—family-of-origin, friends, lifestyle—and there is nothing and no one to help me recreate those moments of communion and connection". She felt out of touch with the world today. It was a deep longing for a time and place long gone, with nothing in the present moment to console. So, on this particularly beautiful late summer day, since Mom was having a 'good day', I suggested that we go on an outing. We would visit Mothers childhood home and the cemetery where so many of her dear relatives lie in waiting...for her.

We hooked Mom up to her 'traveling' oxygen tank, put her little 'Cadillac' walker in the back seat, and off we went on a great adventure! I took along a bouquet of cut flowers, a gift from her Granddaughter, to place on graves as a way of honoring their presence, reminding Mother that these were the people waiting for her on the other side.

We started at the most important, and difficult; Dad's grave site. Since Mom could not get out of the car, I drove as close to his tombstone as I dared. We both greeted Dad, reminding him of what he already knew—she was coming home. I took the flowers she selected from the bouquet and place them at his grave for her. This was the hardest stop of the day, and the longest. I waited until she finished praying, weeping and silently staring into a place I was not allowed. When she came back to the present moment, we moved on.

We went to her home church cemetery and found the grave of her real mother, Caroline. The tombstone acknowledged her untimely death. It was my first encounter with her Mother; a very moving experience for me too. Flowers, prayers of gratitude and a few funny memories recounted and on we went. I would ask Mother who she would like to visit next. Slowly she started to name family, relatives, and friends, starting with her Father and Step-Mother, Sister, and then a host of other characters in her life. I would ask for a story about them, and they were usually precious or humorous. She did not pick out any people who had left a bad memory. Some of the tombstones were easy to find, while others took a bit of hunting. For over an hour she would call a name, and like a rabbit scurrying amongst the leaves, I went searching from one end of the cemetery to the other with her sitting in the car, door wide open, soft breeze blowing and sun streaming into her upturned face. By the time we finished the cemetery was a living reminder of *all* of these every day saints waiting for her arrival; little bunches of flowers were everywhere! What a reunion that would be!!

By now Mother was exhausted, so I took her to an old haunt, a roadside diner that made really greasy and delicious hamburgers and fries. I ordered her one, along with the milk shake she was craving, and we parked the car under a shade tree and broke bread (er.. hamburger buns) together. She did not each much, but just the fact that she could hold it, smell it and savor the memory was feast in itself.

I let her nap for a bit, and then it was time to finish this odyssey to her past. We drove past her first home, the place of her childhood. She told stories about the big sheltering tree she would rest by on her two-mile walk to school on a cold snowy day. I heard tales about herding cattle, playing in the hay, and how her cousin told her the story of 'the birds and the bees' using clover flowers to explain the whole thing.

And then, she suddenly remembered a stream that was her favorite place—she would skinny dip in it with her girlfriends and neighbors. We drove to the old bridge, and underneath was a patch of overgrown grasses and reeds. Her face dropped with disappointment, and then she remarked that even that old creek had dried up. I said, "Not so fast Mom. Let's see if there is anything left of it".

The unusual foliage hinted that some form of water might still be there. Slowly I waded through the tall grass...and there at the bottom of it all was a small trickle of water still running. I pulled aside the grass so the stream was visible and drove the car to the edge of the bridge. "Surprise Mom—it's still here"! She opened that big left eye and—she saw it! Her excitement was profound as tears of recognition and comfort streamed down her ashen face. She had seen enough. It was time to go home and rest in the knowledge that a whole cemetery of ordinary every-day saints—family who loved and raised her through the years—like that little stream, would be there for her when she went home.

Exercises in Generativity

Exploring your ancestry is the starting point for your intergenerational journey. Knowing your roots forms the container that provides meaning for your own life experiences. It is the reference point, the landscape, the nest from which you emerged to enter the world.

Where Do You Come From?

The roots of your origins are where many of the foundational assumptions that guide your expectations and choices are laid; these were the rules for acceptance and survival. Many times they were simply passed down as 'this is how we do things here' and we blindly adopted them without thoughtful examination.   To bring them into your conscious awareness, some questions to explore with the patient might include the following:

- Who are your ancestors—what's the story?

- Where are they from?

- What was their migratory pattern? (It is interesting to note how they got to the place where you were born)

- Why did they move?

- What were their occupations? How did they establish themselves in the land you now inhabit?

- Or… did they stay in one place? What made them choose to stay?

- Who are the hero's, the characters in the family?

- What makes them stand out? (Sometimes it is the black sheep that is trying to break out of dysfunctional patterns, and thus gets labeled by the rest who fear what such a change could mean for the whole group).

- What are the nicknames of key players in your family? What did the names mean and how were they acquired?

- What kind of celebrations and rituals were vital to the culture?

- Or….if you were adopted, what is the essence of that story? (There are no accidents in life. Native Spiritual Healer, Wanagi Waci, shares the worldview of his tribe—'family' is a matter of spirit and heartfelt connection, not a matter of blood relation.

For many Native People, family is a sacred commitment made by a group of spirits before birth. It is simply a matter of 'showing up' at the appropriate time on our life journey to share in the unfolding story that informs and shapes our soul.)

This reflective process provides a good time to visit with the patient and other family members still living that remember some of the characters in the fabric of your family-of-origin story. Interview people who knew them. Gather old photographs and bring them to the patient to be identified. Trace migratory patterns through ancestral treasures and shipping lists. Visit the towns or countries they lived in. FEEL the essence of who and what they were, what of them remains within your family today.

Your Place in the Family

If the dying person is a family member, it is very healing for both of you to identify what you see as the potential for your family's future based on the antics and patterns uncovered. To more clearly identify your 'immediate family' patterns, look at your own.

Draw your family tree (going back2-3 generations), but instead of simply mapping out names and faces, add unusual or striking attributes or life circumstance to the names of people who hold a special place (positive or negative) in your family tree.

- Who are the people three generations back (you are #4)?

- How did these folks navigate their lives? Note the patterns of movement, of occupation, of illness or disease, of relationship in your great/grand/parents.

- Who in the family are you most un/like? Listen to other family members say "You are just like ____" if you really want to know.

- What individual/family patterns do you most resonate with?

- What things are most difficult for you within your family? Often it is in that space that the true 'growth of Soul' material resides.

- How does your family history un/consciously inform your expectations about the path and outcome of your own life?

As we become increasingly clear about strengths and challenges embedded within our family-of-origin, we can build on the power of our heritage, and recognize areas that may pose a potential challenge if ignored. Awareness of our history is the best way to harness and utilize the strengths family has to offer us and our children's futures.

Reflections on Caregiving

The Patient Speaks:
"Leo was in the last stages of liver cancer. When he came to the office, he looked egg-yoke yellow. He reported that a hoped-for decision was not possible, that his ex-wife was already closing in for part of his estate that his lawyer had said, "Don't worry, you're basically bankrupt," and that the pain was becoming intolerable. For some reason my spontaneous response was, "Other than that, how's your week been?" I was immediately concerned I had been inappropriate. However, Leo was laughing so hard I could hardly understand him as he said, "Thank goodness, someone still thinks I am alive! I am so tired of everyone treating everything so seriously!"

Ronna—Patient's Physician

The Caregiver Speaks:
"As people who are ministering to those facing life-and-death issues every day, we doctors are privileged to be in a position to benefit from the hard-won wisdom of our patients. The men and women—and children

too—who have looked death in the face, are often those who know most about living. Their message is: "I learned I was going to die and so I decided to live until I died." They interpret their diagnosis not as a sentence but as a message to live. Their mortality is accepted, not seen as a verdict. How few of us know how to do that!"

Bernie Siegel—MD

8 FORGIVENESS:
Releasing Resentments

Forgiveness is both a refuge and a last action to employ when all else fails. As you eliminate old tapes you will create a loving, forgiving inner attitude. As you forgive yourself, you open a space within yourself to move towards what is new, which is the flow of love.

Nearly everyone has been hurt by the actions or words of another at some time in our lives. These wounds can leave lasting feelings of anger, bitterness and even vengeance. Embracing forgiveness, on the other hand, replaces negativity with peace, hope, gratitude and joy.

Forgiveness is a decision to let go of resentment and thoughts of revenge. The act that hurt or offended us may always remain a part of our life, but forgiveness can lessen its grip, helping us focus on other, more positive parts of our life. Forgiveness can even lead to feelings of understanding, empathy and compassion for the one who hurt us, and ultimately for the whole earth.

Forgiveness doesn't mean that we deny the other person's responsibility for hurting us, and it doesn't minimize or justify the wrong. We can forgive the person without excusing the act. Forgiveness brings healthier relationships, greater spiritual and psychological well-being, less stress and hostility, lower blood pressure, fewer symptoms of depression, anxiety and chronic pain while lowering risk of addiction.

When we're hurt by someone we love and trust, we may become angry, sad or confused. If we dwell on hurtful events or situations, grudges filled with resentment and hostility may take root. Allowing negative feelings to crowd out positive feelings, we may find our self swallowed up by our own bitterness or sense of injustice; we repeatedly bring anger and bitterness into every relationship and new experience. Our life may become so wrapped up in the wrong that we can't enjoy the present. We may become depressed or anxious, feeling that our life lacks meaning or purpose, or that we're at odds with our own spiritual beliefs. We may lose valuable and enriching connectedness with others.

Forgiveness is a commitment to a process of change in our perceptions and actions. Moving away from our role as victim, we release the power and control the offending person and situation have had on our life. Letting go of grudges ends the practice of us defining our life by how we have been hurt. This thinking is replaced with peace, compassion and understanding for ourselves and others. True forgiveness is not about getting others to change, it is more about changing our own thoughts and attitudes, moving from resentment to peace within.

A Story of Forgiveness

This is the hardest part of the story to write. You may think, from things shared until now, that Mom and I were inseparable friends. Truth be told, our relationship is only ten years old. It began when our daughter was deathly ill and Mom came to help. Prior to that event, growing up in the same household was painful for both of us. Mother and I were like oil and water; it was a struggle. For you see, Mom was this wonderful and supportive Mennonite woman, and I, alas, I was a very curious and determined child. Rather than playing with dolls I was reading books on philosophy and psychology. While she was snipping flowers for the church I was looking at slides of cells under my tiny microscope. And, while she accepted things as they were given, I had to check out the meaning behind the baptism vows before I donned the requisite white dress. In short, she did not understand me and I was not eager to follow her lead (which at that time looked like passive accommodation). Why this is such a happy story is the fact that we DID find our way to a common ground, which grew to become one of the deepest loves of my life. And—I will live happily ever after!

So, back to her story. It was several days after our trip to the cemetery, and a full week since she had told me the 'Jam Story'. She was having a 'good day' again, and that little left eye was wide open! Today, I thought, I am going to explore her mind a bit deeper—it holds so much wisdom for me. "Mother", I began as we engaged our morning coffee ritual, " I want to ask you a question. When did you start to discover your own voice, your own power? I realize that was a big step because Mennonite dolls don't have faces—'women are to be seen and not heard'".

She sat thoughtfully, hugging her coffee cup, and then that familiar little chuckle welled up in her throat. "You know, Josey, I think the first time I really spoke out boldly to your Dad was at the time of his retirement. I am a late morning person; I hate nothing more than to be rushed in the morning. But at the same time, I am a late night person. Sometimes I will stay up until midnight if interesting things are going on."

"So Mom, what is 'an interesting thing' to you?" I interrupted. I had wondered how, at age 90, she structured her days in such a way that she was still aware, alert of mind, and selectively engaged in the world and things within it. "Well", she continued, "I start every day with my very favorite breakfast—bread and cheese and some cantaloupe (she was German after all!). Then I pick up my reading".

NOTE: when Mom died I found her notebook listing the 300+ books she had read in the last few years. This interest came into her life when she lost her ability to be out amongst the people. The more homebound she became, the more she read. Reading was her love, her passion. It took her into another world, a world alive with people, intrigue, passion and drama. Our conversations were as much about her current novel characters as her family's current affairs. When her eyesight failed I got her a NOOK because you could make the font larger. She learned how to navigate the technology and read at least 5 books every two weeks for the last years of her life. We were now sharing one of the great passions of my own life.

She continued, "If I am reading a good book, sometimes I don't even get out of my pajamas and will read all day! If the book isn't that good, I put it down after making myself read a few chapters, and then I do handiwork, Word Find or jigsaw puzzles, or watch my favorite TV shows". Now some people watch soap operas but my mother went directly to the source of all love—she watched 'The Bachelor', religiously. Seeing 'young love' unfold gave her great joy. In fact, was well known that Monday evening the phone went off the hook so she would not be disturbed in its viewing! She also loved 'Dancing with the Stars' so that she could complain about the scanty costumes. This was how Mom created her days, putting stimulating thoughts and restful crafting into each day, depending on her level of energy and interest.

"So Mom, how does this early morning person thing relate to you and Dad?" I prodded, bringing her back to the original question. "Oh!" she exclaimed, "I had my days routine all worked out and then your Dad retired. I told him the first day he was home that he was welcome to do anything he wanted, in any way he wanted. He just should not look for breakfast at 7AM, nor ask me to do anything until at least 10:00. He was on his own until then!

And, one more thing—while I was happy that he was now home, I needed my space. So we agreed that if he was out in his woodworking shop I was not to step in and interrupt him. By the same token, if I was in my sewing room, I was off limits to him as well"! I chuckled at the thought of these two strong-willed people having such a clarifying, boundary-setting conversation.

I was really quite stunned, actually! This was not the 'passive accommodation' I had witnessed, or believed I was seeing in mom when I was a child. "Mom, that's fantastic! I mean, that was a bold and outrageous thing for you to do—given your history and our culture." She smiled gently, and then added, "You know, I think it was the final step that led up to the 'Jam Story' a few years later. Taking my power and finding my own voice was a journey I did not start until you kids were gone. I just didn't have the energy or the courage to do it back then."

We both sat in silence thinking of her journey towards authenticity, and my childhood with her. Suddenly she turned to me and said, "Parents always learn so much from their children. I watched you and your sisters do and say things I would never have dreamed of. And then I saw your lives unfold in ways I always had dreamed of. A parent makes a lot of mistakes in their life, but my biggest regret is this—". She stopped mid sentence, took a deep breath, gently lifted my face towards hers and with tears streaming down her face she said, "Josey, I am so sorry I was so hard on you when you were a child. I simply did not understand you. Can you forgive me?" That giant invisible elephant sitting on the table between us had been named.

Stunned and raw in my own memory of what that comment had opened up, I replied, "I am sorry too, Mom. I am sorry that I was such a challenge to raise, and that I did not always understand you either." Mom continued, "As we have been having these conversations, I am seeing myself and my life in a different, a more noble way. Suddenly I realized that you and I are more alike than we are different. We both have the courage of our convictions!" I quickly replied, "And Mom, where do you think I got that trait from?" We both laughed in relief, recognition and—for the first time—total communion of the soul.

And thus began the greatest love affair of my life.

Exercises in Forgiveness

The way to express or experience forgiveness is to recognize its value and importance in our life at a given time. Neither Mom nor I were ready to address the painful, ever present fact that we had spent most of our lives in separation, and frequently, resentment, until that moment of opening and honesty as she approached her passing. It is NEVER too late to forgive others and ourselves.

Practicing the Art of Forgiveness

The act of forgiving begins when you can honestly reflect on the facts of the situation clearly, without adding or taking away anything.

- After examining the issue, reflect on how you reacted, and how this pattern of behavior has affected your life, health and well-being.

- When you are ready, actively choose to forgive the person who has offended you. Stepping out of the victim role, you may also note your own role in the event, how you may have participated in events that led to or set up the situation. You may also observe your own reactions, and how, if the situation was repetitive, you helped to keep the cycle going. This will release the power and control the other holds over you in your memory—and current reality.

- Once this opening occurs, the hurtful experience finds a rightful place, not the place of prominence in your life.

- Staying with it long enough, the final step of healing is a sense of understanding and deep compassion for all involved.

- Remember, forgiveness is something you choose to do, whether the other person agrees with it or not. It's not about the other person, it's about removing the pain and sting from your own memory.

When our daughter had a near-death experience Mother came to stay with her. I saw her express love to Kristi that I personally had never experienced. Seeing her capacity to care so deeply, and realizing that Kristi was the recipient of something I had never known, I decided to forgive Mom and put all that behind us because of its impact on Kristi's life. When I changed my attitude, the journey towards this healing conversation began—it was 11 years prior to the date of this forgiving exchange.

The Creation of Meaning

We must understand our history or we are destined to repeat it. This requires us to reflect on the events of our life and ascribe meaning to them. Meaning is the way people interpret a life experience to deepen their perspective and grow. It is a process that allows us to understand the role of the event in the larger landscape of our lives.

As I continue to sort through the things learned with Mother those last years, and the final, glorious last weeks of her life, three specific responses to the event appear to have been most helpful.

- *Surrender to the moment*—Initially I harbored many painful childhood memories of harsh words and judgment from Mom. I also was acutely aware of my harsh and judging reactions to her presence. As two strong Mennonite women, we had kept struggling against what was occurring, and much energy was wasted in that way. After Kristi's near-death experience (Kristi was a 30 year old new mother at the time) I reflected on Mom's own experience of death in childbirth—loss of her own mother, in a new way. She never had a Mother to teach her how to be present, patient and long-suffering. She was bounced amongst relatives—each taking their 'turn'.

- In the long night hours shared between Kristi and Mom, Mother told Kristi that her nickname 'Jimmy' (her real name was Florence) came from the neighborhood aunts who named her after a newspaper cartoon "Jimmy the Orphan". Mom had only discovered that as the last Aunt told it to her in her passing several years earlier. She had never shared that with anyone until she sat with Kristi and saw Kristi's own intense suffering during the events surrounding childbirth. This opened a new insight for me. And from that moment on I developed a deeper understanding and compassion for my mother. I dropped the struggle 'against her', and blessed the events that had formed her re/actions so deeply. It was what it was, she had survived and evolved into this amazing and loving being sitting in front of me today.

- My friend, Native Spiritual Healer Wanigi Waci teaches that we must make friends with the things that trouble us most. When we embrace them rather than reject them, they become a part of us and the lessons alter our conscious awareness. We soften and open—the space in our body that harbored resentment is filled with love and we become more whole.

- *Acknowledge the emotions*—After Kristi's experience I made a conscious decision to work through this issue with my Mother. I owned and sorted through the deep and disturbing emotions fostered by years of judgment and rejection on both sides. This exercise was the most difficult part of the entire experience for me. It literally forced me to look at things we had experienced across our shared life journey, revisiting things between us that had been hurtful; a lack of 'being there' at some critical time, moments missed because of busyness or inattention, comments hurriedly made that were misinterpreted. Many private tears were shed in those moments of reflection, but they fell away instantly the moment she asked for, and extended, forgiveness. It was a moment of completion for us both.

- Current research supports the fact that emotions create bodily responses at the cellular level. If we acknowledge the emotion, it is 'experienced' and released. However, if we ignore or 'stuff it', it stays buried in the cell, causing a blockage of energy that ultimately leads to bodily illness. Unreleased emotions will connect and vibrate with other similar emotions, events over time. That is why sometimes a seemingly small

70

issue can evoke a profound response. We may say 'where did THAT come from?'

- A strong reaction of any kind is intended to prompt you to ask, "Where have I experienced this feeling before? When was the first time I can remember feeling it?" Such a process guides us to past similar moments that created assumptions, reactions and expectations that have become part of our pattern of behavior. While some of these behaviors are helpful, others may have outlived their usefulness. Replacing them with more helpful, conscious reactions fosters healing at the deepest level of being. Reaching out to others involved in the event to express compassion or offer forgiveness completes the circle of wholeness.

Today is a good day! Both Mom and I moved through the end of her life a little lighter, a little freer, and a whole lot more aware. New insights and capacities gained from this life-long pattern forgiven (on both sides) enriched every aspect of our lives, and we both wish the same for you.

- *Compassion*—Whenever I go somewhere and see someone with inter-generational issues of any kind, I think of how that could have been the outcome of this situation for our family in general, and me in particular, if we had not shared that cup of coffee and exchange. It makes me feel an empathetic at-oneness with the other person.

- *Gratitude*—True gratitude moves us from thanks-giving to a life of thanks-living. Each day has become such a joy! Prior to this final exchange over the issue we both kept a bit of 'pretend' between us—like 'all is well'. As a result of the profound and honest conversation, we both became totally transparent. Nothing more was hidden or ignored; everything had been revealed. There was no more judgment, hiding, or resentment. We were simply 'present' to each other and every moment that transpired. From that moment on, I truly 'knew' my mother. That honest and open connection guided me in what she was to need, every moment in the last days of her life. We had become one. What a wonderful, unexpected, and totally appreciated outcome for both of us!

As we come to know ourselves, we suddenly see the collective Self. And, in that space, all the petty differences, the minor altercations, the myriad set of man-made rules become irrelevant. As we experience the freedom, the joy, the beauty of coming home to our-Selves we can offer that same right to others. While still making judgments about issues in our own lives, we quit being judge over others. The interconnectedness between all is seen and wholeness is experienced.

Reflections on Caregiving

The Patient Speaks:
"When I ask you to listen to me and you start giving advice, you have not done what I asked, nor heard what I need. When I ask you to listen to me and you begin to tell me why I shouldn't feel that way, you are trampling on my feelings. When I ask you to listen to me and you feel you have to do something to solve my problem's you have failed me—strange as that may seem. When you do something for me that I can and need to do for myself, you contribute to me seeming fearful and weak. So, please listen and just hear me. And if you want to talk, let's plan for your turn, and then I promise I'll listen to you."

John—Patient

The Caregiver Speaks:
"Being addicted to helping is so common, yet it is one of those problems seldom discussed. If I were addicted to drugs or alcohol, I'd have groups like AA and substance abuse treatment programs to help me. If I were addicted to food or gambling, or even sex, there would be people sharing

my problem, to accept and help me break free. But there are no Messiah Anonymous groups waiting for us Messiahs. Why not? We are all too busy pretending we have no problems, too busy focusing on everyone else's addiction, to face our own and to offer genuine help to each other. I'm sorry."

Carmen—Nurse (or JoEllen, a Daughter)

9 GENEROSITY
Purposeful Giving

Relating with others and sharing in activities surrounds you with group awareness. Things exist only in relationship; outside of relationship there is no-thing. Reaching out to others enlarges your life through participation and mutual exchange in groups, partnerships and community.

Generosity is the habit of giving freely without expecting anything in return. It can involve offering time, assets or talents to aid someone in need. It is comprised of many small acts of kindness that can leave a lasting impression on all they touch. It is doing the right thing', the doing of a good deed without needing the world to know about it. In fact, most often it goes unnoticed—expect to the one receiving the blessed offering in love from an unguarded heart.

This spontaneous offering is often extended to someone unknown, or hardly known. The origin of this gift springs from that which inspires good and sharing outside the immediate circle of family and friends. It does not require great skill, only deep caring—paying good deeds forward. Doing something kind for another person makes the world a more generous place. It is the balancing antidote to the greed which flows freely through the halls of corporate and political America today.

Hospitality takes this a step further, showing respect for one's guests, providing for their needs and treating them as equals. A loving heart shows hospitality to strangers as opposed to personal friends and family members only. Anyone can be great because anyone can serve. But true non-discriminatory service is the last uncrowded place. All you need is a heart full of grace and a soul generated by love. THAT is why it is such a difficult space to occupy. The Dali Lama observed that, "Our greatest duty and our main responsibility is to help others. But please, if you can't help them, would you please not hurt them. " He was describing my Mother.

A Story of Generosity

Now Mom was an extra-ordinarily ordinary person—at least on the surface. She had an education that spanned from country school to the Teachers Certificate she earned at Freeman Junior College. Beautiful in her own right, she never won a Beauty Pageant. And as she aged, her physical appearance and dress style would not have won her a cover shot of Vogue Magazine. By the world's standards, Mother was a typical 'aging woman' in rural America.

Oh ye with eyes who cannot see—what you did NOT recognize was the size and scope of her heart and its resultant capacity to care, and to share every last thing she had. She was a force for service to the community; an icon of stewardship with her resources in a way that makes the 'Green Movement' pale by comparison. If she did not invent, she certainly defined the notion 'unto the least of these'. Mom was a powerful energy behind the generosity expressed on this planet. Period.

Now such a bold statement demands reinforcement with facts How many people do you know that quilt over 100 quilts and *give* them all away to bless a worthy cause (a quilt the quality of Mother's usually took the better part of a year—start to finish—she had several going at all times). She also cooked up a storm or created a contribution for every single community event—Hospital Auxiliary Soup Day, Freeman Junior College Schmeckfest, Work Day at the North Church, Mennonite Central Committee state-wide sale annually. This never stopped her from making countless individual wall hangings embroider sets of tea towels for Freeman Community Hospital, kni bandages for Women In Missions in the Mennonite Central Office

Mom shared her many talents, limited resources and unending imagination with simply anyone who crossed her path that showed the smallest inkling of a need or interest in her services and support—on a grand scale!

However, what was most compelling and precious about Mother was the way she tended to the individual. Since her death—which has been several months—we STILL continue to get notes and testimonials regarding the way SHE was the one that first invited them into her home for a meal when they joined the church, lost a mate, moved to a new and scary place; changed focus in their life in any way. Mom had a parade, a literal cast of characters, through her home across the span of her life. She demonstrated this innate sense of recognizing what people needed most to heal the wound of their heart that change had wrought, and she was first and foremost a champion of the broken-hearted. I believe this deep sensitivity arose from the abandonment she experienced at her birth.

So fast forward to this, the final chapter in her life. Mother had limited, but precious, resources. She had given so much away that only her deepest treasures remained in that little apartment. When we took her home she stated that the *one thing* she wanted before she died was throw a party! In the less-than-perfect way a mere mortal works, we looked at the calendar. This was August. She would move into the Assisted Living apartment on September 1st (her demand). So, she wanted a celebratory gathering at her home on the eve of August 31st —her last act of independence before moving to institutional care.

By her decree, it was to be a two-fold event. First, all the granddaughters and the mothers (we sisters) would meet with her. She had serious things to discuss and gifts for us all. After that, we would eat a light lunch and then invite our FAVORITE Aunt—Faye Goertz—and her daughters, Linda, Brenda and Jenny, to sip a bit of wine and celebrate the life we had all shared together for more than half-a-century. The next day, mother would move to the institution. So she had planned for this event to occur—Wednesday, August 31. Perfect.

Now the problem we 'mere mortals' face is the fact that there is a force beyond our own that truly guides our destiny. And *that force* showed us another reality. As the days of late August appeared, instead of stabilizing and moving towards independence, Mother was losing ground—fast. However, she was so fiercely independent that she refused assistance. Each night as I would put her to bed she would disgustedly remove the oxygen mask, nestle under the bed covers, and settle into 'sleep'. Since she had severe Congestive Heart Failure, her lungs would quickly fill up, forcing her to change position. Around 1:30 AM she would get up, find her 'Cadillac' walker and motor off to the bathroom, then settling in her beloved brown chair for the remainder of the night.

Knowing that the one thing that would totally derail her plan for "death by completion' would be a broken hip, the moment she fell asleep in her bed, I would make a nest on the floor at the foot of her bed and rest; waiting for her to awaken for that journey of independence to the bathroom. At the first sound of her stirring I would slip outside the room and then walk in as though her movement had captured my attention. TOGETHER we would navigate to the bathroom and then, her chair.

On a Friday night, mid-August, a most dreaded thing occurred, she lost consciousness. I had just gotten her from bathroom to chair when she convulsed, seized, and quit breathing. I thought she had passed, prayed her soul to the other side—when suddenly—quite abruptly, she started to breathe, the left eye opened wide—she was back!

As she regained consciousness I asked her, "Mother , what is left on your list you need to complete" (realizing that there was something of unfinished business that had called her back). "I want to see Paulie one more time" she replied. Paulie, the beloved sister from Colorado who dutifully and lovingly had made her annual odyssey home to Freeman from Colorado every year since she left home 25 years ago. Paulie, the daughter that faithfully watched 'The Bachelor' and 'Dancing with the Stars' so that she could call after the event and compare notes on how each of them had voted. Though separated by miles, Paulie was a heartbeat away! Mom was waiting to say goodbye to this, her beloved daughter.

I freshened mother up, put her to rest in her much-loved chair, and walked outside. I needed air and nature to re-balance from the difficult witnessing of her unconscious episode that had just transpired. *Immediately* the phone rang—divine intervention. It was Paulie (who had plans to travel to Freeman in time for the 'Wednesday party') inquiring into the status of my mother! I shared that the only thing left on my Mother's 'completion list' was seeing her again. "Honestly sis", I advised, "I am not sure she will still be here on Wednesday. She is starting to move between the worlds. If you want to experience this amazing woman that Mother is becoming, can you come sooner?" " I will jump in the car and be there tomorrow" was her immediate and compassionate response.

Bernie and Paulie are twin sisters. They were the pride, the very glory of my mother's life on earth. Aside from having her first born show up as a son (in those days boys, like bulls in the cattle market, had more value), birthing twins gave my mother bragging rights. Only Marty Kaufman had pulled off a similar feat. Twins somehow brought distinction to a woman and her tribe! Paulie graduated from college, married her sweetheart and moved to Colorado. She was always an adventuresome creative, fiercely independent and totally outrageous woman with a sense of humor that would serve us well in the final hours of Mothers life. Secretly Mom drew her strength from Paulie's raw courage and authentic presence.

Bernie, on the other hand, was the Social Director of the Universe—bubbling, vivacious, and cheerleader of humanity! She was interpersonally gifted—the world was drawn to, and celebrated her presence…..and she was MOST like Mom. Everyone loved Bernie. We were often told that 'every family needed a Bernie." Like Mom, she had the gifts of hospitality and creativity, enlightening and lifting community wherever she went. There was a natural affinity between Mom and Bernie; they were made of the same cloth. So, Bernie had always been Mother's main-stay, her rock.   Paulie and I were a bit more on the periphery—an icon of what might also be possible—but not so acceptable by social standards. Bernie lived only a hundred miles away and was frequently in and out of Mothers' long and exciting life with perfect timing. She was the one who helped me physically manage Mom through the month of August, and, much to my eternal gratitude, was very instrumental in helping keep Mom at home. She was scheduled to return to Freeman on Sunday, after she finished church obligations.

Paulie drove the long trip from Denver to Freeman non-stop. She arrived at Mom's bedside on Saturday afternoon to a cheerful and tearful reunion. The following afternoon Bernie arrived. Now, all three were present and accounted for. After assessing Mother and her capacity, we jointly decided to move the party from Wednesday to Monday. We called everyone invited, and happily, all could shift their schedule. Monday was set for 'give-away' day.

Sunday night the inevitable occurred. Getting Mom up to the bathroom, she arrested again. Together we gently lowered her to the floor. After a long period of 'being gone' she returned—left eye wide awake. With unbelievable determination she helped us get her back to her beloved chair. Once she was settled and sleeping I told my sisters, "We cannot take care of her alone any longer. We must get some form of help." So the next morning I called my friend, Dorothy, one of the finest Hospice Nurses in the region.

As I explained our plight to Dorothy, she agreed that it was time to move Mother's status from Palliative Care to Hospice. Mid-day Monday Dorothy appeared with a wheel chair to help move Mom from place to place, a bedside commode that would help us with her bathroom needs right beside her well-worn chair, and comfort measures such as mouth care swabs, cleaning cloths for a soft bath, and Morphine for to take the edge off her pain. Mom was quickly moving to the end of her life.

At 5 PM sharp the party began! Her granddaughters, Kristi, Marsha and Kathleen, appeared. We had freshened Mother up and gotten her into the wheelchair, wheeling it front and center into her spacious apartment living room. Mom looked radiant! She was beaming with joy as we manufactured each remaining quilt, afghan, picture, dish or other memorable treasure of her heart. Each gift she had selected had a story about a trip with Dad, a loving contribution from someone she had supported in one way or another. Over a period of almost two hours she disposed of the things most important to her, savoring the delight and appreciation of the women who loved her most.

After a bit of dinner, the door opened and Faye and her daughters arrived! Now the noise and excitement rose to a new level. Faye's grand daughter had just been married in Jamaica. Not being an alcohol-prone family, Faye brought the bottle of rum she had gotten as a souvenir. She busily made Pina Colada drinks for everyone in the room—strong on the ice, soft on the rum. Mother simply loved them. She had not eaten in a few days and the cool smoothness of the drink was a total delight to her. In fact, she not only finished hers, she polished off Paulie's as well! Little did we know that would be the last food she would ever enjoy.

Aside from the stories and laughter we always shared with our cousins of more than 50 years, Mom continued to give to them some of the things she had been saving. Emotion was raw. Tears flowed freely, and love and gratitude filled the room. It was a perfect party! After almost three hours, I looked at Mother, who was now exhausted and said, "Mom, do you think we should put you back to bed?" to which she promptly and crisply replied, "Don't rush me!" I laughed uproariously….she was still in charge.

After the last person left and only the grand/daughters remained, she said, "Let's just sit a minute." In the growing silence we sat with Mom as she savored this moment of fellowship and re-union. After a small window of silence, she asked to go back to her chair, and it was the last time Mother ever got up again.

Exercises in Generosity

Throughout our life all of us gather up treasures of the heart. It may be things, such as a collection of precious dishes or jewelry, or documents such as cards and letters sent from others. We may be avid readers and acquire a library of books. Whatever it is, there comes a time when we must consider how to dispose of those assets upon our departure.

Planning the Give-Away

To eliminate a struggle between relatives and friends who want a memory of you through your personal items, write a letter of planning if you can't have a party. By actually inviting those closest to you over, as Mother did, you can lay out the items and allow the individuals to select those most precious to them. In this way you enjoy not only their appreciation, but also see what it is that they value most.

If direct gifting is not possible, be mindful of the stories we all have heard regarding 'relative fights' over how to divide the family pictures, necklaces, stamp collection, or the wedding gift from Uncle Bill. The items may have more sentimental than monetary value, but getting them to the right person can make a big difference to you—and to them (the little pig salt and pepper shakers were an item of great value at this particular give-away). If you want to make sure that your granddaughter gets the pearl necklace you got for your high school graduation, or you have already promised your best friend that she gets your figurine collection, put your wishes in your letter. Also, be sure to leave instructions about care for your pets.

Leaving A Message of Love

Make your gifting personal, too. You can use your letter to send important messages to your survivors. You might include special hopes you have for your grandchildren's education, or the important values you want to pass. While Mom did not have a significant amount of money, she designated the cash received when her parents died to her great-grandchildren (of which she had 14!). She had a file in her financial affairs with a note attached to the investment account created from her own Mother's gift. It read:

> *"I've been thinking! I will not put my money in stocks or bonds that have such a low interest rate - Instead thru the next 2 years I'll invest in my precious great grandchildren - to start their college funds. May it grow with you. Then spend it wisely and may all your dreams come true!"*

82

Mom was truly caring for seven-generations.

Reflections on Caregiving

The Patient Speaks:

"I know you feel insecure, don't know what to say, don't know what to do. But please believe me, if you care, you can't go wrong. Just admit that you care. That is really what we are searching for. We may ask for whys and wherefores, but we don't really expect answers. Don't run away— wait—all I want to know is that there will be someone to hold my hand when I need it. I am afraid—I have lots I wish we could talk about. It really would not take much more of your time…if only we could be honest, both admit our fears, touch one another. If you really care, would you lose so much of your valuable professionalism if you even cried with me? Just person to person? Then it might not be so hard to die—in a hospital—with friends close by.

Carrie—Dying Student Nurse

The Caregiver Speaks:

"If you want to help a person—including yourself—giving until it hurts, you need to take into account some deep-seated reasons why most caregivers can't stop giving, even when they become ill themselves. Ignoring these underlying psychological factors is like trying to pull a tree out of the ground without taking into account the extensive roots that keep the tree firmly in place."

Leonard—Counselor

10 TRANSCENDENCE:
Peaceful passing

Today is a good day to die for all the things of my life are present.
Crazy Horse, Native American Healer

Intellectually and scientifically, death is defined as the cessation of bodily function that sustains a living organism. The body simply stops. Death by this definition is very mechanical, predictable, an end-state in and of itself. Transcendence, on the other hand, is a spiritual term that represents a state of being that surpasses mere physical existence. It typically implies a state of being that goes beyond the mere body into a state of being that includes the divine, in both knowledge and being. It resides beyond the grasp of the human mind, but remains within and beyond the mysterious bounds of the Universe.

Being raised a Mennonite in a very strict and traditional faith, my understanding of what Mother experienced in the last twenty-four hours of her life is best described by the term transcendence. In this view the sacred is all around us. Instead of heaven being a destination, heaven also can be experienced whenever we have eyes to see the subtle beauty and presence of what is good and true and beautiful in the earth; in relationships, in activities, in solitude. Let me explain:

A Story of Transcendence

After the 'great give away party' we wheeled an exhausted and exhilarated Mother back to her beloved chair. Now she just loved

85

that chair—because it 'fit'. A stocky German Sherman Tank body does not fit just any piece of furniture. This glorious chair was short; it accommodated all of her 5' 1" frame. It was also ample; it was as wide as it was high. Mom could pour her abundant body into its embracing arms, while also having a foot rest that was just the right length to accommodate short outstretched legs, and a head rest that lovingly embraced a short stocky neck. It was perfect! And so, in the final days of her life, it became her refuge; her sanctuary for the body, mind and spirit.

Along with that, having the love and concern of her three daughters surrounding her gave her the sense of deep security emotionally. We had been together throughout her life. For the first eighteen years, in her presence, and, upon completion of college, we all made it a high priority to stay connected in whatever way worked, given the circumstances of our life. Mom *knew* that she was loved. And we, in turn, knew she loved us too.

At age 80 we introduced her to e-mail and the computer. Though she struggled at first, she would not give up. She quickly conquered the technology, her driving motive being that she was able to remain connected to the 'whole family'. We set up her internet address book, but the only one she used faithfully was the one marked 'family'. From this post she would connect, communicate and cheer for the family of her heart—members of her immediate family, and often times, extended family.

And so it was that Mother, our great connector, was now in a failing position. The desire to 'live in her own home until she passed into the sunset to become a memory' was becoming quite a real possibility. Truly, her body was moving fast towards end-of-life! She had the diagnosis pressed upon her on August 6, and here it was, August 30. Doing the great work she had done emotionally and spiritually (for so much of the past few years), her 'to do' list had been cleared. Her financial and every-day life activities had been wiped clean. All that was left now was the daunting task of releasing this weary and worn body, and float to heaven and the spirits waiting on the other side.

After her party finished we put Mom to rest in her chair. At 3AM she awoke, tried to get up to the commode and arrested once again

We struggled to get her back to bed, and then realized she would never leave her chair again. Working through that painful realization is best done when surrounded by the sisters of your heart. Together we reflected on what was happening, what would be the next 'best steps' and how to proceed.

And suddenly—the morning sun arrived. Dorothy called to check on us. I explained the current situation physiologically so she came to remove things no longer needed. Twenty-four hours after Hospice equipment arrived, it was removed. Gone was the wheelchair needed to escort the Queen to her Court of adoring children and grandchildren in the glorious give-away of the evening before. Gone was the commode that held her ailing body when she had to relieve herself. All that was left was Mother, her Daughters, and the oxygen machine humming quietly in the background.

Dorothy very gently gave us instructions on how to remain steadfast at Mothers side, assuring us that the end was drawing near. She also said that it would be in our best interest to 'take shifts' so that rest could occur for us in our long and oftentimes painful vigil. We all nodded in agreement, but never, not for one second after the third daughter arrived, did the three of us ever spend a moment apart. One for all and all for one was our motto. We were here for Mother and for each other, to support the most eloquent passing that Mother could experience.

Tuesday was a long day of vigilance. She was drifting in and out of consciousness. I reminded my sisters that she was attending orientation to heaven" when she was in that space of in-between. She awoke mid-afternoon, delighted when Kyle & Kahler, the great grandchildren who grew up at her kitchen table, came by to show their support. By late afternoon she was not aroused.

Suddenly, the phone rang--it was 8:30 PM. It was Ethan, one of her Great-grandchildren. "Grandma", he said to me. "I can't sleep and I am so sad about Grandma TJ" (they knew her as the grandmother with the Shiatsu dog named TJ—whom she had lost a few years earlier). " Can I tell her I love her?", inquired this 13 year old young man. "Absolutely" I replied! I quickly took the phone and placed it at Mother's ear. "Mom", I gently called, "Ethan wants to tell you he loves you." She struggled to return to consciousness, opened that left eye, and smiled broadly as Ethan delivered his message of love to her.

We hung up the phone, and two minutes later it rang again. This time it was Josh, an 11 year old Great-grandson of Grandma TJ. With the same request, we took the phone once again to Mom, and she whispered, "I love you to JJ".

The phone was barely in its cradle when the phone rang a third time. It was Brandon, a grandson from Colorado who had thoughts of Mom and wanted to tell her of his affection and appreciation for her. The phone pressed to her ear, Mom smiling and whispering "I love you too Brandy."

Again the phone rang, this time it was Mike. He, like the other cousins, had sensed a need to connect with Mother and share his love and support. His timing was perfect. It was as if this event had been orchestrated by a force outside ourselves.

Once again the phone was replaced in its cradle only to ring again! Five phone calls within 15 minutes!! What was happening? This time it was the call she had been waiting for all day—it was her son Dick. As he told Mom how much she had meant to him through the years, her smile broadened, her body relaxed deeply, and when we hung up after this good-bye, she lapsed into a deep, deep sleep.

We three sisters spent all night watching at Mothers side. At times we would sing to Mother (sorry Mom, we did not want to keep you awake through annoyance, we wanted to help you remember earlier years when our trio was actually pretty good!). We played her favorite CD classical music. We told stories in front of her, laughing uproariously at some of the antics of our youth, or her recent behaviors and attitudes that would both shock and delight us. Sometimes we would weep, raw and open, telling her how much we loved her and how much she meant to us. Each of us took our turn dipping in the relentless grief that sweeps over one in waves as they realize that they are saying good-bye to this unfathomable treasure of their life.

As Wednesday morning moved towards noon, her body covered with perspiration, Mother opened her eyes once again. The wide open left eye surveyed the room, left—center—right. We were all there and accounted for! She smiled in relief and settled back into her chair. The three of us decided to give her a bath. While Mother had been modest all of her life, she had no energy for modesty now. She relaxed into our efforts to wash and bathe this ample and beautiful body. Three warm washcloths in a ritual of sanctification. Three loving presence—with Paulie assuring Mom, "don't worry Mom, we are not looking!" Mom startled us all with a quick quip, "There is nothing here you have not seen before!". Laughter filled the room as we offered this sacrament of cleansing to her dying body. (Later a Hospice nurse friend told me that by doing that for her she was able to conserve just enough energy for her final transition—remember energy is the guide for all you do with/for the dying person).

After we gave her a backrub, offered mouth care and a sip of Morphine, she settled back into her chair, looking glorious in her clean robe and freshly brushed hair. She looked at Bernie, beckoning her forward and gave her a kiss. She looked at Paulie, calling her close and gave her a kiss. She looked deeply into my eyes likewise, drew me too her and offered a kiss. My sister said, "Mom, are you afraid to die?" She said, "No!" "Then Mother, why are you still here?" she inquired. Mom looked so lovingly at each of us, "Because you are", was her reply. In that statement I realized that while Mom never was able to experience the total and unconditional love of a Mother in her birth moment because of the illness and passing of her own Mother, in this instant she was savoring the unconditional love that flows between family when the fullness of the relationship is realized. We were the midwives and mother for Mom as she moved into her new home in heaven.

Mom settled back into her chair, struggling for breath. Suddenly she reappeared, looked left, center, right to check if we were still here. Smiling softly she looked at each of us saying in that moment saying, "My precious daughters…..thank you, thank you, thank you." Those were the last words exchanged between us.

Mid-afternoon Wednesday arrived and Mothers body was still here—struggling for each breath. Her awareness had passed on. We were still in our pajamas as we had not left her side since the party on Monday evening. Exhaustion, a deep aversion to watching her struggle for air, and the fear that if this did not end soon she would need institutional care; we were beside ourselves. Then a small miracle occurred! Suddenly the door opened and Dr. Kirtin arrived. This beloved Hospice physician had ridden his bike over to make a house call (he used rubber bands to hold his pant legs close to his ankle so they would not get tangled in the bike chain mechanism).

He came in and sat beside Mother's dying body, looked at each of our exhausted and tear-stained faces and gave what we would later affectionately refer to as *"The Dr. Kirtin Death Speech"*. He started by commenting on the good job we had done keeping Mother comfortable and clean. He then, in his gentle way, started to address each thing we had been most worried about (*how* did he know these were our concerns—had he been eves-dropping??)

"Don't worry about your mother's labored breathing", he said as he went on to explain how the body adjusts to deep congestive heart failure. Her 'struggle for breath' was not as difficult as it was adaptive to her changing lung mechanics. We discovered that her breathing pattern was more upsetting to us than to her.

He went on, "Now remember that you are angry and have many targets for it. But the root of all your anger is the fact that your Mother is dying. You may be wanting to start to go through her things, but fear that it is disloyal to her (had he heard us debate if we should remove the picture of her beloved TJ from the refrigerator as we were cleaning, or leave it in case she would be alert when she moved out so she would see it right where she had left it).

You should begin to take turns sitting at her side. And don't worry if you are not there at the moment of her passing: *THE SCRIPT HAS ALREADY BEEN WRITTEN*. She knows you are here. She feels your love. You have given her the gift of dying in her home. And now, it would be appropriate to take the oxygen from her face, it is irritating to her" And with that he gently removed the face mask that had been such an annoyance to her since her return from the hospital several week earlier.

He encouraged us to play music, continue the morphine and simply be present to her and each other in the hours and days ahead And with that, he was gone.

How peaceful Mother looked without that oxygen mask! How relaxed her body became. Within twenty minutes of his departure, she graciously exited her body. Her life was ended. The three of us standing around the bed looked at each other. We looked at the clock. We looked out the window. 5:15 and days end was approaching. We called Dorothy in Hospice and she came to fill out the death papers which I, as Healthcare Power of Attorney, signed. We called the Funeral Home of her choice and twenty minutes later they came to pick up her body. As they rolled her out of her little apartment we saw the sun begin to set.

Mom had died at sunset, just as she requested. She died two days after the anniversary of her husband's death 15 years earlier. She died 6 days before her 91st birthday. She died the eve before she was scheduled to move into institutional care.

We danced. We swirled and 'high fived' each other. We jumped and giggled with glee. Mom had done it!! She had orchestrated and navigated her death experience in a period of 25 days. And in that experience, we all became more whole.

Mom's death certificate reads: "Death by Completion".

Exercises in Transcendence

Once Mother had passed, funeral arrangements were the next order of business. But, that was not a daunting task because, true to her style, she had a carefully planned set of instructions we took to the Funeral Director the next day.

Funeral Arrangements

The little tin box with her funeral arrangements included the following items:

Mom had indicated what Funeral Home she wanted to handle her affairs.

She also listed the names and contact information of special people she wanted to be told that she had passed away

The box included the type of funeral arrangements she wanted:

- She identified what type of burial she wanted (while Dad had been cremated this was NOT something she wanted, so a traditional burial was planned)

- She planned for her grandchildren to be pallbearers and the great-grandchildren would release balloons at her grave site (there had to be a job for everyone)

- She had identified what songs she wanted sung, including a copy of the arrangement just as she had wanted it

- She had not paid for the funeral arrangements, but had left money in her bank account to cover expenses (if you pre-pay make sure that this is noted in your instructions)

- Her burial plot had already been purchased when Dad passed away; her deepest desire to lay next to him would now be realized

- Mom stated that she wanted a certain amount of her remaining assets to go to the 'Organ Fund' at the Salem Zion Church

- Mom had written her obituary (which we updated since it had been drafted 26 years earlier—how is that for thinking ahead!!!

- She even had a copy of the poem she wanted in the back of her funeral program, as well as thank you notes for the people who showed up to celebrate her passing

Mom had so carefully thought through the mechanics of her funeral that all we had to do was select the dress she would wear and the coffin that would host her precious body. In the month of August, when we still though she might go into Assisted Living, we helped her finish a beautiful quilt and pillow for her 'new home'. Since she was going to heaven instead, we draped her simple wood coffin with the quilted masterpiece, rested her head on the pillow, placing a simple bouquet of red roses on top. This plain but beautiful elegance was the perfect tribute to the woman we were honoring.

Including All Family Members—Near and Far

My brother, firstborn in the family, lives in Alaska. Those first several years of his life were spent with Mother and the Grandfathers, as Dad was a soldier in WW II, serving his country. While mom loved all of us 'best' she had loved him 'first and fiercely'. Through the years he kept phone calls and messages flowing. The connection between them never altered. The night before Mother passed, his call was the crowning glory to her; the final communication she took by phone. In that exchange she told him what a wonderful son he had been and how much she loved him. The feeling was mutual. So, on the occasion of this funeral his absence was keenly felt.

Thanks to the wonders of technology, during the wake the night before the funeral, and during the funeral itself, I continued to take pictures with my cell phone in real-time and send them to Dick, who was sitting in front of his computer. The church graciously taped her ceremony and uploaded it onto the web upon its completion. So he went to the link to hear the specifics of the event as soon as it was over.

During the ceremony we wanted Dick to be actively present. So he and his wife Karen participated in writing the tribute we gave to Mother during the ceremony. It read:

Tribute to Florence Goertz—Our Mother

We are all born of mothers. Some of us are lucky enough to be born of moms. My sisters and I are among the most fortunate to have been raised by our mom – Florence "Jimmy" Goertz.

Although I am unable to be with you today to share in person my thoughts and memories about mom, please know that I am certainly there in spirit. For all of you who knew mom you will understand exactly what that means. Mom had more 'spirit' than any person I've ever met. It was her faith in family that kept her strong throughout her almost 91 years.

South Dakota was the center of her universe – her place to always call home. From there she and dad traveled the world where she was fascinated by the many different cultures and peoples. This gave her an understanding of the universe. She brought this back to her home and incorporated it into her life.

Even before my "memories" really began, it was her strength that shone through. My parents were separated by the responsibilities of duty to country before my birth. While my dad served in World War II overseas, mom lived through much of her pregnancy and my birth alone, save for the loving care of my grandparents. Before dad returned from the war, she managed to find an old country farm house and have it transported to Freeman by horse to be set up on 7th and Dewald Street. From there the Reuben Goertz family grew and created its own legacy. Over the next few years the family added my sisters: Joey, Bernie and Paulie. Eventually each of us married and expanded the world with mom's grandchildren and then great-grands.

Our early years were spent as many of you of my generation might remember. The town was our playground; the county our birthright. Grandparents lived "down the street". "Dress clothes" were mended and patched until they were finally relegated to the "play clothes" shelf. Anything serviceable after that was shared with cousins and friends or remembered once again when plucked from the "rag bag" for use. Pleasures were of the homegrown variety. "plicking" peas from our garden, enjoying "homemade" German food like nalles nicki, berogg knepp, kuchen, poppy seed rolls, or on special occasions—chislic!

Maybe we couldn't have "store" bought bread like some; but there was always homemade bread available. We bought "bologna ends" from the butcher and dined like kings. "Christmas candy" found its way into cookies and cakes long into the following year. Holidays were spent with family where my grandparents looked on as the cousins raced around the house, played cards, or worked on jigsaw puzzles. Maybe we couldn't vacation to exotic lands but the family car took us and our little tent to see America. I doubt it was as crowded as mom's apartment must have seemed to my sisters her last few days.

There is something to be said that in a time of "make-do" our parents made sure that each of us attended college, going on to create our own careers. We know that she loved us all. She had the strength to set us free to follow our dreams while she provided us each with hand-sewn quilts to keep us safe and warm.

The hardest thing Mom experienced throughout her life was saying good-bye. Each farewell, no matter for how long a period or for what distance, brought quiet tears and a quivering of her lower lip along with hugs and embraces. In my last phone call with her this week she told me: "I love you, Dick." Mom, I love your too.

After reading Dick's comments, I continued:

On August 6, mom was admitted to the hospital for a few days, only to discover that she could not stay home alone. When the doctor asked what her desires were for the treatment of her health challenge, she said:

"You know in a few weeks I'll become 91 years old. I've had a good life. Reuben and I lived it to the full and had a great time doing it. When I'd get ready to go to Bible Study he'd jokingly say—you're cramming for the finals. I guess the time is here, sooner than I had expected. So my wish is to be kept comfortable. When my time comes just let me go into the sunset and become a memory."

Her deepest desire was to die in the comfort of her own home surrounded by family. We had the profound privilege and honor to grant her this one last wish, and she died at home at 5:15 Wednesday, the evening before she was scheduled to move to the Salem Home. Her death certificate reads—"Death by Completion".

Mom, we love you dearly.

Reflections on Caregiving

The Patient Speaks:
"Placing my illness in a spiritual perspective in no way diminishes what you offer us from your training, experience, individuality, special skills or sense of humor. Quite the reverse. Your particular talents and unique qualities come forth more reliably when you have a richer and more spacious sense of who you are—the very promise of all spiritual practices.

Louise—Patient

The Caregiver Speaks:
"The reward, the real grace of conscious service...is the opportunity not only to help relieve suffering but to grow in wisdom, experience greater unity, and have a good time while doing it!"

Dorothy—Family Member

AFTER-WORD

After Mother passed I received a poem from Wanigi Waci, the Lakota Spiritual Holy Man who had so lovingly tended to Kristi in her near-death experience. He had been sending notes of encouragement throughout her last month of life.

In the Lakota Way an Elder holds a special place in the life of a family. They believe that the spirit of a young child and an elder are connected in a special way because the fontanel (soft spot on a baby's head) is open in both age groups, and the spirit moves more freely in and out of the body. Communication and communion between young and old are more direct.

On the occasion of Mother's passing he sent the following poem:

For my beautiful friend Jo Ellen and her Sisters on the rebirth of her mother back into Soul in Creator's time.

Ina tokiya ilala he
Ochichile tja hehanesh elyaunshni
NiTunkashila (Wakan Tanka) wa nicho chi yagnikte elo
Mother, where have you gone?
I look for you but you are not here
God has called you
So you have gone home!
Mother where have you gone?
An ache so deep has replaced your touch, your soft whisper, your smiling eyes and your breath,
The many untold and unfathomable spirit connections engulfing my thoughts of you,

To try to speak of them would be like trying to hold the energy of neutrinos from the atoms,

What I see, things I hear, ways I feel , memories I smell and nourishment I taste has the essence of you,

God has called you

So you have mended an earth circle of life and transcended back home. Mother where have you gone?

I see you in everything and sense you here, I look at our grand and great grandchildren, I see you at play,

I look in my daughter and I see you starting the un-fold-ment of womanhood, generation of replenishment,

I look in the mirror and I see beauty of me and you, meyou, youme us, we, and .....I!

As I take on the weight lifted from your shoulders I pray you will help to uplift my heart as a shining beacon of hope, charity and love,

Though we wear the skinclothing and place of responsibility in motherhood, grand-motherhood and great grandmamma

I commitment to let God shine through as you did and continue to do,

I am you,

As you are I,

In the completeness of our children and their many children' children to come.

Today I come to realize heaven is in my heart and the memory door to eternity that holds the sacred key to God's love.

Your daughters that you know,
Jo and her Sisters

ABOUT THE AUTHORS

Florence Caroline Goertz was a Mom of extra-ordinary capacity! She raised four children, guided eleven grandchildren and supported fourteen great-grandchildren. In her creative life she quilted, embroidered, wove, crocheted, knit and sewed more beautiful gifts than can be counted. Her artistic ability was matched by her sense of hospitality with enough baked cakes and casseroles to feed a multitude. But the best quality of this amazing woman was—she found meaning and beauty in the ordinary every-day things in life. Every day was a moment to celebrate!

JoEllen Goertz Koerner, RN, PhD, FAAN, has been a lifelong recipient of her mother's advice and guidance (usually appreciated). She also lived in Freeman, raising twin children on a 4th generation farm/ranch operation. Her professional background is filled with a variety of experiences from healthcare administration and education to regulation in many diverse healthcare settings – hospitals, healthcare systems, ambulatory and home care are just a few. She served as president of the American Organization of Nurse Executives, receiving their Lifetime Achievement Award for Patient Care Education & Research. Dr. Koerner then moved into an entrepreneurial career on the world wide web, creating teaching tools and strategies that empower people to manage their own health using holistic principles. It was this background that prepared her to witness and support her mother's passing. JoEllen can be reached at www.mylifecanvas.com

OTHER BOOKS BY THE AUTHOR

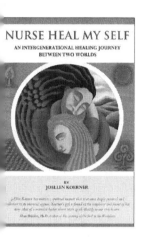

Mother Heal Myself: An Intergenerational Healing Journey Between Two Worlds.

Renowned nurse executive, JoEllen Koerner, presents a stirring account of how ceremonies of the Lakota Sioux tribe healed her daughter after Western medicine had failed. More than an autobiography, *Mother, Heal MySelf* is a deep exploration of the meaning of healing and how it is practiced successfully in multiple valid healing systems.

Healing Presence: The Essence of Nursing

In this new edition, JoEllen Koerner explores the intersection of scientific, creative, and spiritual ways of knowing that inform and inspire "healing presence" in caregiver and patient. Revised, updated, and refocused, the book integrates traditional nursing practice with cutting-edge alternative and integrative medicine. The author expands our' awareness of Allopathic and alternative ways of healing as rooted in Native Healing

ractices. The book also explores new models for transpersonal caring hrough the lens of philosophy, spirituality, and complexity science. It is a profoundly important resource for nurse educators, students, and practitioners. Order Online: www.springerpub.com

Healing Presence Card Deck

A set of 36 uniquely illustrated cards represent various aspects of the human condition. They are constructed by layering multiple related illustrations, one on top of the other, to portray a striking image which projects the vibrational essence of its content—Visual Homeopathy. Viewing the card and reading its related text promotes deeply meaningful personal reflection into your Self and the meaning and purpose of your life. The cards can be used alone, or with someone who is struggling or suffering with personal/health issues in their own life.